SHANNO

See Yourself as God Does

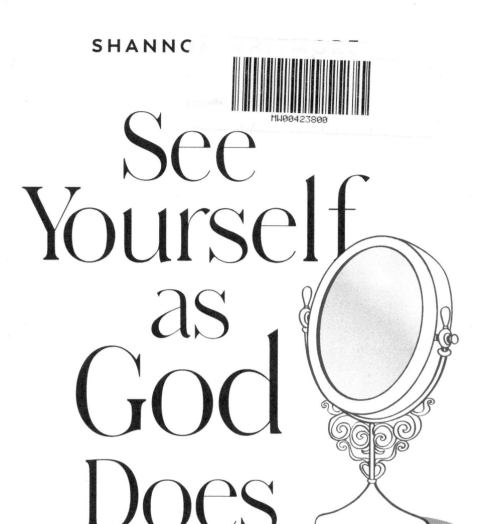

Understanding Holy Body Image
Through Catholic Scripture

ASCENSION

West Chester, Pennsylvania

Ascension
PO Box 1990
West Chester, PA 19380
1-800-376-0520

Cover Design: Teresa Ranck

Printed in the United States of America
23 24 25 26 27 5 4 3 2 1
ISBN 978-1-954881-92-1 (paperback)
ISBN 978-1-954881-97-6 (e-book)

Contents

Introduction 1

PART 1: YOU ARE BEAUTIFUL

Chapter 1: The Creation of Man 11

Chapter 2: God's Vision for the Body 27

Chapter 3: Motherhood and the Body 41

PART 2: YOU ARE BROKEN

Chapter 4: The Fall of Man 61

Chapter 5: Our Broken Bodies 79

Chapter 6: Motherhood in a Fallen World 95

PART 3: YOU ARE BLESSED

Chapter 7: The Redemption of Man 111

Chapter 8: The Body Redeemed and Restored 125

Chapter 9: The Great Gift of Motherhood 141

Conclusion 155

Acknowledgments 161

Further Reading 163

Introduction

I spent nearly a decade in hiding. If we had passed each other on the street, you probably would have thought I was just a normal girl. I was slim, but not "skinny," and I ate more than just naked lettuce leaves for lunch. I never talked about my weight, and I never said no when someone offered me cake. I never acted like what I considered to be the stereotypical "person with an eating disorder." I was totally normal. My normal BMI even told me so. I used that label as justification for my situation. So how could I have an eating disorder?

I had spent a childhood mercifully free of body image issues. By middle school, I was awkward in my body, as most adolescents are, but I still felt comfortable with it. I enjoyed sports like softball and figure skating and had a fast metabolism. I never gave any consideration to what I ate, and I was naively unaware of the war that was brewing just beyond the horizon.

I was still stick thin and curveless when I began high school, but puberty finally struck during my junior year, and my body became completely foreign to me. I was uncomfortable with my new curves, and I tried my hardest to hide them beneath baggy T-shirts and loose-fitting pants while I became better acquainted with my new body. I had always enjoyed playing sports, but now I couldn't run as fast, and my hips always seemed to get in the way. Guys seemed to like my new curves, but I spent most of my time wishing my body would go back to the way it had looked before puberty.

Puberty looks different for everyone, but most girls will feel like they're living in foreign bodies at some point or another. Some girls shoot up like weeds. Others develop acne that scars their faces. Some develop large breasts, while others gain wide hips. Puberty affects us all, whether we want to be changed by it or not. I would have rather stayed thin and boyish in appearance, but that just wasn't in the cards for me.

I would have preferred to live unnoticed as I adjusted to my larger, curvier form, but I wasn't very successful. It began with an ill-considered comment, a comparison voiced by a girl who was probably just hoping to feel better about herself. I don't remember what we were discussing, or how this comparison even came up in conversation, but a classmate made a comment that implied that the way I looked was not aligned with the "beauty" standards of the day. I was mortified. I was even more dumbfounded when no one bothered to correct her for criticizing my body. That was the first time I heard the lie whispered in my ear, *You're too fat to be loved.* From that day forward, I never saw beauty when I saw my body. I saw something unattractive that needed to be changed if I was ever going to be loved.

Thus began a decade of body image issues that culminated in an eating disorder in my early twenties. I have prayed for that young woman often in the years that followed that careless comment. I'm sure she had heard the lies too, and she was probably just as broken then as I would become. If you listen to the lies long enough, you start to believe them, and once you start believing them, it's only a matter of time until they break you. In the years that followed, I was broken again and again, until I was sure that I was so shattered that I was beyond the possibility of healing. But I didn't know the power of the Healer yet.

Ironically, my relationship with God began just as my relationship with food and exercise began to fall apart. I was a junior in high school when I attended my first retreat voluntarily, but that was also the year I started sneaking diet pills. Throughout college and grad school, I gave talks to teen girls on beauty and self-respect all over the East Coast, but I was secretly skipping meals and punishing myself with intense workouts regularly. In my case, I hit rock bottom during one of the most spiritually uplifting points of my life. I was twenty-four years old and studying to become a religious sister (a vocation that did not pan out). I spent my days in prayer and service, but my nights were spent binging foods in the privacy of my own bedroom. The sheer dichotomy of my life was just what I needed to recognize the truth. I was ashamed and realized that I had been living a lie, and I was ready to face the truth. And the first truth that I needed to accept? You can't pray all your problems away. Faith does not exempt you from suffering.

The road of recovery has been long and winding, with some shortcuts and a few detours, but I know where I am going now. My destination is heaven. My destination is Christ. But he is also my traveling companion. I have finally come to understand what God has been trying to tell me all along. Prayer has been essential to my healing, but it wasn't enough on its own. I couldn't just pray away my disordered habits, and it took a combination of faith, education in nutrition and exercise, and a lot of emotional support from friends and family to find the healing I needed.

My struggles began with the whispered lie that I was not pretty enough. I was too fat to be beautiful. You don't need to suffer with an eating disorder to hear that lie whispered in your ear. The more women I talk to, the more convinced I become that most women hear that same lie and believe it. We believe that something about us makes us ugly, makes us unlovable. We all might have different struggles, but so much of our suffering can be traced back to the same lie. We believe that we can only be loved if we are beautiful and that we are just too ugly to be worthy of the love of God. But that's a lie. It's simply untrue. Healing means ignoring the lies and learning to hear the truth—we are all beautiful.

WHY THIS BOOK IS NEEDED

I struggled for a long time to understand the relationship between my faith, my inaccurate view of perfection and beauty, and my discomfort with my body. On the one hand, I assumed that if I prayed hard enough, the struggling would just fade away. On the other, I expected that the deeper my faith became, the more perfect I would become. And I wanted nothing more than to be perfect.

Like many women who want to see themselves as beautiful, I tried to be perfect. Perfect grades. Perfect hair. Perfect skin. Perfect reputation. Perfect body. Perfect me. I wanted to be perfect. And didn't God want me to be perfect? Didn't he specifically pray that we would be perfect as our heavenly Father is perfect? Wasn't I just trying to do what God wanted me to do? To be what God wanted me to be?

It took me about a decade to understand that God's definition of perfection and mine were very different. It took me even longer to understand the proper relationship between health and wellness, the desire to be beautiful, and my personal faith. How was I supposed to find balance when I was surrounded by such a diversity of believers, ranging from paleo-dieting Catholics to those who seemed to live by the motto "you only live once"? How would I know if I had slipped back into obsessive workouts when seemingly healthy believers suggested that they couldn't live without a daily workout? Was focusing on makeup and clothing akin to vanity, or was it appropriate for women to accentuate the beautiful bodies they had been given? Was it pride or gratitude to want to look pretty? And what is health anyway? What is beauty? What is perfection? Without the answers to those questions, I was lost. But as I continued to practice my faith and, more importantly, study it, I finally began to find the answers I had been searching for.

I've read some wonderful self-help books about body image and eating disorders. I've even stumbled across one or two Catholic ones over the years. But none of them was able to quite do it for me. I consumed them like the starving soul I was, but none of them provided the theological foundation I needed to connect my heart and my head. I accepted that God loved me. I accepted that God found me beautiful. I accepted that God wanted me to be healthy and holy. But I didn't know why. I didn't know what it really meant. And without answers to those fundamental questions, I could only travel so far on my journey toward healing.

I found the key to recovery in St. John Paul II's Theology of the Body. I finally figured out how to interpret that key through my own experience of marriage and family life. And after finally finding the answers I had been searching for, I knew that I needed to share them. I needed to share the wisdom of St. John Paul II's life-changing theology, wisdom that finally provided healing to my wounded soul. But his words were not mere self-help literature or some New Age philosophy for overcoming eating disorders. It was Truth himself. It was the divine Word entering my heart. It was the Great Healer, guiding me through the revolutionary teaching of a saint. God spoke to me through the words and wisdom of St. John Paul II, and I finally found the answer to all of my prayers, even those I had not had the energy or wisdom to pray myself.

If you have ever struggled to see yourself as beautiful, this is the book for you. If you've ever been confused about the relationship between you and your body, this is the book for you. If you've grappled with the idea that your body is a gift from God, and therefore good, this is the book for you. If you have suffered from an eating disorder and you've struggled to find answers, this is the book for you. If you are still wading through the waters of early recovery, unsatisfied with the self-help books you've been reading, this is the book for you. If you've been walking the road to physical healing for a while now but still feel like you're spiritually empty, this is the book for you. This is the book I longed for in my own journey to healing, and since I couldn't find it, I wrote it. In addition, Julie Matsen, a licensed psychologist specializing in body image, has created practical exercises that you can find at the end of each chapter to help you see yourself as God does.

I pray that you find some of your answers here. I pray that you find the words to express the things you've been feeling in your heart. I pray that you open your beautiful heart to the Lord so that he might speak the words of life into it. I pray that you find peace.

God wants you to believe you are beautiful. He wants you to know you are perfectly made and worthy of love. You are God's wonderful masterpiece, created in beauty, broken by sin, and blessed by the Lord himself in the plan of redemption. God doesn't make mistakes. He works miracles. God is the divine artist who fashioned each of us in love. He created us good and beautiful. But then we mucked it up. We rejected his love, and we were broken under the weight of sin and death. God's greatest work of art shattered in the midst of a fallen world. But that wasn't the end of the story.

God loved us too much to leave us broken. So he remade us, washing us clean in the blood of Christ. He collected all the pieces of his broken masterpiece, and he created something new. His original work of art was beautiful, but now it is glorious. His original vision was perfect, but now it is a stained glass masterpiece that reflects the very light of Christ. Redeemed mankind has become a reflection of the divine. You are a reflection of the divine. Now it's time for you to start seeing yourself as the perfect masterpiece that you are.

Part 1

· · · · · · · · ·

YOU ARE
BEAUTIFUL

1

The Creation of Man

At the lowest point in my struggle with an eating disorder, I was convinced that the only way for me to be "better" was if I could maintain my shaky grip on control at all times. Food was the enemy, a necessary evil, and a major source of temptation. Food wanted me to fall. It wanted me to fail, to lose control, to give in and let go. I only felt like I was succeeding in life when I was controlling how much I ate and when. And when I inevitably failed? I tried to find redemption by regaining control through punishment. I considered it a type of mortification—if I ran a few extra miles or cut out carbs for a day, I would be in control again. I would be better. I would be closer to perfection.

You might not consider food to be the enemy. Maybe it's the fashion industry for you. Maybe it's how only certain body types are represented in television, movies, and advertisements. Maybe it's the constantly changing fads that you just don't have the time, money, or energy to keep up with. There are countless "enemies" out there, apparent roadblocks in the path to perfection. They exist purely to trip us up, to remind us that we are not as beautiful or perfect as we want to be. In a woman's quest for flawless perfection, there is always an "enemy" to face. There is always a battle to be fought and most likely lost.

I tried really hard to save myself. I thought that if I was disciplined enough, I would be able to resist the temptation to binge when I felt tired, unhappy, or dissatisfied. I thought that if I just avoided those "occasions of sin"—if I slept ten hours a night (because the more time I spent asleep, the less time there was for eating); if I kept myself busy with school, work, and extracurricular activities; if I refused to buy any food besides what I absolutely needed to survive—I would be able to save myself. But it was too hard, and I was not "good" enough. So inevitably, before the day was over, I would give in to the temptation and binge again. I would tell myself that this was the last time, that I would feel better after I was done, and that I could start fresh tomorrow. Tomorrow was always another day, but I spent too many tomorrows living in the torturous cycle of binging and purging. Because inevitably tomorrow would come, I would wake up feeling awful and hating myself, and the cycle would continue. I lived through countless tomorrows, but I never accepted the grace needed to start anew. Time and again, I punished myself rather than forgiving myself and starting fresh. When what I really needed to do was let go, all I could do was hold on tight to my weak sense of self-control as I tried to save myself.

During my first year as a graduate student, I lived in a boarding house for young women. Every night, I returned home from classes or work to find my dinner waiting for me. I would throw out half of the food before sitting down to eat what was left of the meal. And as I ate, I would stare at the various baked goods piled high on the dining room table. Inevitably, there were cakes, cookies, or breads there, just waiting to tempt me. They were donations from the local bakery, and I considered them to be my worst enemy. On a good night, I could eat my meal quickly before running off to my room. But from time to time, I would cave in to the temptation to have just one bite. But then one bite would become two, two would become ten, ten would become half the cake, and if I could stop myself in time, I would throw out the rest of the cake and return to my room, hot faced with shame. The enemy had caught me in its clutches again.

But the truth? Food might have been a source of temptation for me, but it wasn't evil. Food was meant to provide nourishment to my body, but I often turned to food for comfort. I fell for the lie that food would heal my inner brokenness, but I was turning food into something it was not. Food was not evil. It was not the enemy. Food was not trying to destroy me. It also wasn't trying to fix me. Food could not heal me. It wasn't going to ever satisfy me in the way I longed to be filled. Eating food would never make me feel better and neither would starving myself to regain control. But it took me a long time to realize that. It took me years to realize that God was the comfort I sought, that his was the healing I needed. Only God would ever truly satisfy me, and only he could redeem my brokenness. I couldn't do it myself. I wasn't meant to do it myself. I was supposed to let go, hand over my desperate need for control, and allow God to enter into my brokenness and transform it.

A pivotal part of my healing process was accepting that food was not an enemy out to get me. Food and exercise had huge parts to play in my personal struggles with my body, but food is not the "enemy" for everyone. Not everyone will define beauty the same way. For some, the "enemy" is the fashion industry, with its constantly shifting ideals of what counts as "beautiful." For others, the "enemy" is the makeup and clothes used to hide blemishes and imperfections of the skin. For still others, the Enemy might use women in their lives as temptations to think that other people are beautiful but they are not. We all have "enemies," but they are just the smoke screens projected by the true enemy. We all have the same enemy—Satan. And we all have the same Savior—Jesus Christ.

THE FIRST CREATION STORY

> *Then God said, "Let us make man in our image, after our likeness; and let them have dominion over the fish of the sea, and over the birds of the air, and over the cattle, and over all the earth, and over every creeping thing that creeps upon the earth."*
>
> *So God created man in his own image; in the image of God he created him; male and female he created them.*
>
> *And God blessed them, and God said to them, "Be fruitful and multiply, and fill the earth and subdue it; and have dominion over the fish of the sea and over the birds of the air and over every living thing that moves upon the earth."*
>
> *And God said, "Behold, I have given you every plant yielding seed which is upon the face of all the earth, and every tree with seed in its fruit; you shall have them for food." (Genesis 1:26-29)*

The first pages of Genesis are probably some of the most well-known passages in the entire Bible. I read them in my first-grade religion class, my tenth-grade Hebrew Scriptures class, and my master's level Old Testament class. You just can't study the

Catholic Faith without reading the story of Creation. It's just too foundational. We can't understand Christianity (or Judaism for that matter) without becoming familiar with the first three chapters of Genesis. We can't understand what it means to be a human being without those chapters either. We can't fully understand who we are until we know what we were made for. And we can't fully appreciate where we are going if we don't know where we have been. The two accounts of Creation provide answers to some of the most fundamental questions of human existence: What is man? Why was I created? What is my purpose in life?

If your religious education has been a bit spotty, or if it has just been a while and you need to brush up on your Bible knowledge, here's a quick breakdown of the first three chapters of Genesis. In the first chapter, you have the traditional six days of Creation, beginning with God creating day and night and ending with the creation of man. We will refer to this as the first account of Creation. In the second chapter, you find a more detailed account of the creation of the first man and woman, Adam and Eve, in the Garden of Eden. This is the second account of Creation. In the third chapter, you read the story of the first temptation, the Fall of man, and his (and her) expulsion from the Garden. For now, we are just going to focus on the first two chapters, but we'll come back to the third chapter in a bit.

MAN AS THE PEAK OF CREATION

The six days of creation follow an upward trajectory, beginning with the most basic foundations and finishing with the highest forms of creation. Beginning with day and night, sky and water, earth and seas, God moves toward more complex creations with each passing day. He gives life to plants and trees, followed by the fish of the sea, birds of the air, and all creatures that live on the earth. Finally, at the end of the sixth day, God reaches the most unique creation of all, man.

At first glance, our creation is the same as that of every other creature. God speaks, and we come to be. We are made out of nothing, like everything else. But this is where the similarities end.

We are created in the image and likeness of God. We are created through the Word, the Son of God. And do you know what that means? The image of God in us does not stop at our souls, at our abilities to choose, think, and love. The image of God in man is made manifest in the body. We were created in the image of Jesus Christ, the second Person of the Trinity, God made man, "the image of the invisible God" (Colossians 1:15). Our bodies are not just temporary holding cells. Our flesh is not just matter. Our bodies have been fashioned in the image of the incarnate Son of God. It's no wonder that after God finishes creating man, he looks upon his newest creation and says that it is very good. When God looks at Adam, he sees his Son.

Mankind is not just a very good creation. We are the point of it all. God spent the first six days of creation preparing the world to welcome us. We are the high point of Creation, the reason God created the world in the first place. He did not need to create the world. He did not need to create man. But God is Love himself, and "God, infinitely perfect and blessed in himself, in a plan of sheer goodness freely created man to make him share in his own blessed life."[1]

GOD'S GOOD GIFT OF CREATION

All of creation is a gift for us. From the beginning, God meant that man should have dominion over the world. He gives us our

---

1   *Catechism of the Catholic Church 1.* All quotes marked CCC are from
     the *Catechism.*

mission in life: Fill the earth and subdue it. Have dominion over all living things. We are meant to be the caretakers of all creation. We are meant to be stewards of all that we have been given. Just like God's love overflowed into his creation of the world and of us, our love is meant to overflow into the world around us.

God never meant us to be at the mercy of merciless creation. We were never supposed to be controlled by the world around us. We were meant to have dominion, and dominion is not about control. Subduing the earth is not about manipulating it, forcing it to do whatever we want. When we're given a gift, the appropriate response is not to crush it beneath our dominating fist, like a toddler with Play-Doh. We're supposed to take care of it. God gave us the entire world as a gift, and we are meant to care for it and treasure it.

Everything that God created is good. That includes everything from our food to our bodies. Creation was never supposed to be about control. Yes, we are called to have dominion over the earth and to subdue it, but we're not supposed to control it. We shouldn't need to. When it was created, we were not at war with the world. We were in communion with it. If we feel that we are at war with the world, with our bodies, or with food, it's because of what came after creation. But we'll come back to that later.

THE SECOND CREATION STORY

Then the LORD God formed man of dust from the ground, and breathed into his nostrils the breath of life; and man became a living soul.

The LORD God took the man and put him in the garden of Eden to till it and keep it.

Then the LORD God said, "It is not good that the man should be alone; I will make him a helper fit for him." So out of the ground the LORD God formed every beast of the field and every bird of the air, and brought them to the man to see what he would call them; and whatever the man called every living creature, that was its name. The man gave names to all cattle, and to the birds of the air, and to every beast of the field; but for the man there was not found a helper fit for him. So the LORD God caused a deep sleep to fall upon the man, and while he slept took one of his ribs and closed up its place with flesh; and the rib which the LORD God had taken from the man he made into a woman and brought her to the man. Then the man said, "This at last is bone of my bones and flesh of my flesh; she shall be called Woman, because she was taken out of Man." (Genesis 2:7, 15, 18–23)

In this second account of Creation, we see God forming Adam, the first man, out of the earth. The implication is the same as in the first story: Adam is made by God. Adam is a creature. His very body is a gift from God, formed and molded by the divine Creator himself.

After Adam is formed, God breathes the breath of life into his nostrils, and he becomes a living being. He was physically alive before this moment, but now Adam is spiritually alive, with the very Spirit of God within him. This is what sets Adam (and later Eve) apart from the rest of creation. From the moment God breathes life into Adam, Adam has a share in God's divine life. He has God living within him. Adam is not merely alive, like the plants and animals around him; he is a living being.

In this account, each animal is presented to Adam as a potential partner for him. During this process, Adam recognizes that while he is a creature like the rest of the animals, he is also different. He stands above the rest of creation, and as a result, Adam is given the opportunity to name each animal as it is brought to him. While he is in communion with all of creation, Adam longs for the type of communion only possible with an equal. So God creates a true partner for Adam.

God casts a deep sleep on Adam before removing a rib from his side. He then fashions Eve from that rib. Adam and Eve are made of the same stuff. Yes, they are made of the same dust, but they also possess the same spirit of God within them. Since God draws Eve from the side of Adam, there can be no question that both man and woman are spiritual beings as well as physical. They are both embodied souls, and their bodies and souls are essential to their humanity.

All humans, like our first parents, are embodied souls. We are not fully human unless we have both. Our bodies and our souls make us who we are. They were created by God, and therefore they are innately good. Our bodies and souls are meant to be reflections of one another. If we strive to cultivate a pure soul filled with God's grace, that grace will be manifest in our very bodies. God's grace within us, shining forth in our bodies, is what makes us beautiful. This is why saints like Mother Teresa, despite being old, wrinkled, and frail, are still beautiful. When people look at them, they see God. They see Beauty himself. We might struggle to see ourselves as beautiful, but if we focus on the beauty of our souls, the world will see our beauty. The world will see his Beauty. And maybe if we focus on our souls, rather than our bodies, we'll learn to see ourselves as beautiful, body and soul, as well.

CALLED BY NAME

Adam and Eve are clearly creatures, fashioned by the hand of God, but they are also set apart from the rest of creation. Once again, we are left with the sense that man and woman have a privileged role among all of creation. God calls man to cultivate and care for creation. God creates man to subdue the earth, to receive it as a gift to be treasured and cared for. God gives Adam authority over the world around him.

Adam is given the task of naming the animals, showing his dominion over them. By naming the animals, Adam has a certain degree of power over them. Man's ability to name and exercise proper authority is a reflection of the power of God. As the prophet Isaiah writes, "I have called you by name, you are mine" (Isaiah 43:1). God was able to call us by name because he knows us, and he knows us because he is our Creator. He formed our inmost being and knit us in our mother's womb. We belong to him.

In an analogous sense, man has power over the rest of creation, and in particular, mothers and fathers have authority over their children, whom they name. Names touch the core of our identity, our very being. This is the reason why my husband and I agonized over the names of our children and why we insisted on finding out our children's genders before they were born. In imitation of God, we were able to call our son and our daughter by name before they were even born. We knew them, we received them in love, and now we exercise our God-given authority over them.

They are ours, but before they are ours, they are God's. Our children existed in the mind of God well before they existed in my womb. God knows my children better than I do, and he loves them better than I do. They were his before they were mine, and they are only mine because God gave them to me first.

I have never struggled to see beauty in my children. I look at them, and I am awed by their freckled noses, their dimpled cheeks, their toothy smiles. I am awed by their beauty. Gazing at my children, I am convinced that God gazes at us in the same way. When he looks at us, he sees our soft curves, our crinkled eyes and smiles, our strong arms and legs, and he is in awe of what he has created. He marvels at all his works. And he invites us to do the same. Each of us is a marvelous work of the Lord, and if we were to see ourselves in the light of the Lord, we would see ourselves as the beautiful pieces of art that we are.

RECOGNIZING THE TRUE ENEMY

In the pages of the first two chapters of Genesis, we are given the blueprint of creation, God's plan for mankind. Had we not fallen, creation would have continued to exist with all the goodness it possessed when it was first made by God. God is all good, and everything he has created is good. We, the peak of creation, are called very good. The world was never meant to be the enemy. Food was never meant to be the enemy. Our bodies were never meant to be the enemy. They are all good things that were given to use as gifts to be treasured and enjoyed. We were not meant to be at war with any of these things—the world, food, or our bodies. They were meant to be gifts.

When my son was born and I took him into my arms for the first time, the nurse smiled at me and said, "Here is your son," before giving him to me. As I held him, I thought about everything that I had already given to him. By giving birth to him, I had already given him flesh and life. But that wasn't all. I had given him the world. In that moment, I remember looking down at my son and thinking, *This is what God must have felt when he created Adam.* God had given Adam flesh and life, but he didn't stop there. He gave Adam the entire world as a gift to be enjoyed. And when I gave birth to my son, I gave him the world as a gift as well. We are all meant to take delight in the world, to enjoy it and take care of it.

The world is ours to take delight in. Our bodies are ours to take delight in, and we can take delight in God's creation through our bodies. When we hear the birds singing or see a rainbow after a storm, God is inviting us to take delight in his creation. When we hold a baby in our arms or hear a child's laughter, God is inviting us to take delight in his creation. When we enjoy a delicious slice of chocolate cake or share cocktails with friends, God is inviting us to take delight in his creation. When we feel our muscles stretch and burn during a hard workout or feel the wind in our faces as we run, God is inviting us to take delight in his creation. But it is up to us to accept the invitation.

God wants us to enjoy the world that he has given us, but it is up to us to decide how we want to receive it. We can choose to receive it with skepticism and distrust, believing that the world is there to tempt and trick us, or we can choose to receive it with childlike joy and faith, as the gift that God intended it to be. God has spoken this world into existence, but our response is our own. We can respond with words of suspicion, or we can choose words of praise and thanksgiving. What we say and what we do is our choice, which is yet another gift that God has given us—our free will. And our free will might be the most complicated gift of all.

The world was created good. Our bodies were created good. Food was created good. If our story had continued in the Garden of Eden, if Adam and Eve had never committed that original sin and been exiled from Paradise, we would still inherently know that. If only Adam and Eve had not been tempted to disobey God, if only man's free will had not led all of humanity down the path of sin and death. But the first two chapters of Genesis are not the end of the story. They are only the beginning, a beautiful beginning that shows us what God always intended for his perfect masterpiece.

QUESTIONS FOR REFLECTION

1. What does it mean to be made in the image of God?

2. How do our bodies help us to reflect God?

3. How did God intend for us to relate to the world around us?

4. How might we better treat the world as a gift to be treasured rather than something to be controlled? How might we better treat our bodies as a gift?

5. What are some of the false "enemies" that you have in your life?

An Exercise in Seeing Yourself as God Does

GRATITUDE FOR THE GIFT OF OUR BODIES

When we struggle to accept our bodies, we often become locked in a battle to change or coerce them into something "better" or "more attractive." We can begin to see our bodies as obstacles to be overcome or problems to be solved. This viewpoint can disconnect us from understanding our bodies as a gift from God, meant to be used as a means to glorify and serve him as we move through the world. Because it is so easy to forget how we ought to relate to our bodies, it is important to cultivate a loving relationship with our bodies, and it can be helpful to thank God often for how our bodies serve us. Consider using the following strategy to help support gratitude and compassion.

1.   Get two sheets of paper. On one sheet of paper make a list of all the meaningful, important things your body has allowed you to do in your life. Think broadly about this. For example, perhaps your body allows you to hug your loved ones, climb the stairs, kneel in prayer, receive Jesus in the Eucharist. Everyone's body has different abilities and challenges. Generate a list that is specific for you.

2. On the other sheet of paper, make a list of actions you can take that show honor and gratitude for the body God has given you. These do not have to be complicated actions. Some example actions you might consider: resting your body when it is tired, spending time in sunlight, and drinking enough water. Again, everyone's body is different. Make a list that is specific to your body and its needs.

3. Get a jar or box. Tear or cut out the individual items on your list, fold them, and place them in the jar. In moments when you are struggling with gratitude toward your body or feel locked in a battle to make it different, take out one of these slips. Add to the jar regularly when you discover something new to be grateful for or another way to care for God's gift.[2]

---

2   Each "Exercise in Seeing Yourself as God Does" has been created by Julie Matsen, PhD, a licensed psychologist specializing in body image, to help you put the chapter's message into practice.

2

God's Vision for the Body

I spent more than a decade feeling like I was at war with my body. It was not thin enough. Not smooth enough. Not strong enough. Not firm enough. It was not enough, and at the same time, it was too much. Too big. Too ungainly. Too scarred. On occasion, I would have something to be "proud" of that seemed to justify my eating disorder—the first time I ran a 5k, prom dress shopping after a week of restricting food, or the occasional compliment from a stranger on the street. But they were just moments scattered over years of self-loathing. Every time I found something to like about my body, I could list ten things I hated about it. And it seemed to hate me too, refusing to do what I wanted it to do.

I wanted my body to cooperate with my desires. I wanted it to be able to run for miles without tiring. I wanted it to move without jiggling. I wanted my body to be slim and toned and smooth. I wanted it to never feel hunger, to never need sustenance. I wanted it to be satisfied with only the smallest of meals, and to never be tempted to eat anything except what was necessary for survival. I demanded so much of my body, but whenever I saw myself, I could only count the ways I had "fallen short"—the thick thighs that touched, the arm flab that seemed to hang from my bones, the curve of my abdomen. I was too much and not enough at the same time.

27

For years, I began each day by standing in front of my bathroom mirror to catalog all my flaws. I listed all the ways I hated my body, all the ways it betrayed me. My body was something to mold, to shape according to my desires, but it constantly fought against my efforts. I ran for miles every day, hoping that I could force my body to be thinner. I avoided sweets in the hopes that my skin would become smoother. I binged and then punished myself later because despite all of my work, my body just wouldn't listen. I felt betrayed by my body, and I hated myself for failing. So I wore baggy clothing to hide my body, because I was ashamed of it. I wore lots of makeup to hide all the blemishes. And I hid from my friends because I didn't want them to think that I was weak. I wanted to be a fighter. I wanted to win. My body was the enemy, and I was at war.

Many women have felt at war with their bodies at one time or another. For many young women, puberty is a period of feeling uncomfortable and unfamiliar with our bodies as they develop. Some girls get hips and breasts, while others get acne. Some grow from pretty little girls into gawky, gangly young women, while others leave behind a childhood of relative obscurity and are thrust into a new world of teenage popularity. Some girls find themselves shopping at thrift stores in the hopes of being stylish despite a lack of funds (or because of parents who just didn't see the need for the latest clothes), while others try desperately to hide beneath layers. Some girls struggle to compete in sports that were once enjoyable, while others become the head cheerleader. Puberty is different for everyone, but it's a rough time for most of us.

And if it's not puberty, it might be later in life, when we become mothers. We gain weight, get bags under our eyes, and have swollen ankles that just won't fit into our favorite shoes anymore.

Our old clothes don't fit anymore. Our old eating habits don't fit anymore. Our bodies don't fit anymore. We hide our bodies in flowing layers of clothing, hide the bags under our eyes with copious amounts of makeup, and hide our swollen ankles with baggy pants and boots. Our bodies once again feel foreign to us, as they change from day to day, week to week, month to month. The changes are inevitable, and we welcome them for the sake of our children, but we fight against them nonetheless.

Many of us have felt betrayed by our changing bodies at some point. For some of us, we have felt at war with our bodies more often than we have been at peace with them. But inevitably, we all grow tired of fighting. I fought for more than a decade because I was ashamed of my body. It took more than ten years before I was finally desperate enough to throw up the white flag of surrender. But it wasn't my body or the world that I was surrendering to—it was God.

NAKED AND UNASHAMED

The man and his wife were both naked, and were not ashamed. (Genesis 2:25)

To be naked and unashamed—it was a concept I just couldn't wrap my head around. If I found my own body to be shameful, how could anyone ever see it any differently? How fortunate Adam and Eve were, to be able to experience the enviable position of being naked and unashamed. When they looked at each other, they saw the totality of the other; they saw who they each were, body and soul. There were no secrets, no reasons to hide. What a glorious, and completely inconceivable, existence—to be naked and unashamed.

I once heard someone say that the only time we can be naked and unashamed is when we are in the shower. I laughed when he said it, but I couldn't help but think, *Yes, that's true.* As a young adult, the only time I felt comfortable with my body was when I was alone in the shower. I felt at peace with my body, content with its curves and planes. I could be naked and unashamed—right up until I stepped out of the shower and came face-to-face with my reflection. The moment I would behold myself in the mirror, the peace would shatter. The contentment would cease. With my body reflected back at me, all I could see were the flaws. But for the time I lingered in the shower, I was blissfully unaware. I could be naked and unashamed just for a moment.

Adam and Eve were created naked and unashamed. At their creation, they were perfect and perfectly attuned to one another. They shared a communion with one another, a relationship rooted in love rather than lust. They experienced a desire to give themselves to the other, to embrace the other and become one. There was no temptation to treat the other as anything less than a person, a beloved child of God. So they could be naked and without shame. There was no reason to hide, and they had nothing to be ashamed of—so very different from our own experience of our bodies.

Adam and Eve's bodies were perfectly united to their souls, and their souls were perfectly attuned to the needs of their bodies. All desires that they experienced were rightly ordered and untouched by sin. Love was free from lust. The consumption of food and drink was unaffected by gluttony. This is what John Paul II calls "original innocence" in his Theology of the Body.[3] Adam and Eve were pure and innocent, their bodies and souls not yet touched by sin.

---

3   John Paul II, *Man and Woman He Created Them: A Theology of the Body,* trans. Michael Waldstein (Boston, Pauline Books and Media: 2006), 18.1. All quotes marked TOB are from this source.

Prior to the Fall, Adam and Eve did not know death. Their bodies were healthy and untouched by the effects of illness or age. Adam and Eve ate when they were hungry and stopped when they were satisfied. When they wanted to walk, their bodies easily carried them, and when they wanted to leap, their bodies effortlessly did it. There was not yet any disconnect between the desires of their souls and the abilities of their bodies. Their bodies and souls were perfectly attuned to one another.

When I think about Adam and Eve in the Garden of Eden, I often think about my children. When I was a new mom, I read somewhere that children will naturally stop eating when they are full. When we repeatedly tell our children to eat faster and finish everything on their plates, we are actually pressuring them to ignore their natural hunger and fullness cues. According to the theory, most children are born with the ability to properly interpret their bodies' signals. Like Adam and Eve in the Garden, they eat when they are hungry and stop when they are full. Most of us are born with this innate ability, but the longer we live in this fallen world, the more opportunities there are for sin to break those natural inclinations.

We can probably all remember how it feels for our bodies to respond to us correctly. My kids leap around with absolute abandon. Their bodies are young and not yet affected by time and age. But their bodies and souls are also more closely aligned. They carry within their souls the burden of original sin until it is removed in Baptism, but their youthful innocence brings with it some of the body-soul unity that Adam and Eve once experienced. Children are a window, somewhat fogged, of what life was like before the Fall. Children are comfortable in their skin; they are at home in their bodies. They have what so many of us want. They are at peace with their bodies. We want that peace, but so many of us find ourselves at war instead.

THE SACRAMENT OF THE BODY

Before the Fall, man experienced perfect communion in all of his relationships. Man was in communion with God. He was in communion with the world. He was in communion with woman. And man was in communion within himself. When man was created, his body and soul were perfectly united. The body was the physical representation of the soul, the visible, touchable reality of the invisible soul within. The body was never just matter, a form that we borrowed for our time on earth. It has always been more than that. Man's soul gives life to the body, and his flesh reflects the soul in a way that can be seen, touched, and heard.

This is why the disfigurement of the human body in any way is immoral. Our bodies are not just flesh to be manipulated, to be cut and refashioned as we see fit. When we alter our bodies in drastic ways that are not medically needed, we are rejecting the body God gave us. We are denying that our body communicates something of ourselves to others. Living in a world that embraces cosmetic surgery, it should come as no surprise that we forget that our bodies are more than just matter to be manipulated. Our bodies are gifts, and they are a key part of what makes us human. The bodily changes that come with puberty, motherhood, and aging should all be viewed as proof of a life well lived, rather than things that need to be changed.

God created the body to be a "sacrament" of the soul, a physical representation of the spiritual reality that lies within, unseen (TOB 19.4). To better understand the meaning of a sacrament, consider a hug, a kiss, or any other act of love. A hug is not just the physical act of wrapping one's arms around another person's torso. A kiss is not just touching one's lips to another's. Hugs and kisses are signs of love. They *really* communicate love. They are the body's way of saying, "I love you." Kisses and hugs are not just physical actions without meaning. They are real, concrete symbols of love. Hugs and kisses signal the deeper truth of love. They are expressions of love.

In the same way, our bodies are expressions of our souls. Our bodies communicate our souls to the world of the senses. They are the exterior representation of our interior being. Our bodies make visible an invisible reality. Our souls are spirit, and therefore invisible, but our bodies are a sign of what the eye cannot see. This is why everyone agrees that Mother Teresa was a beautiful person. She might have been short and wrinkled, but her beautiful soul shown through every iota of her flesh. She was beautiful, inside and out. Bodies and souls are meant to reflect one another. A beautiful soul is reflected in the body. Unfortunately, we live in a world that largely does not believe in the soul, and without a soul, the body is just matter that does not really matter. But that's simply not true. The body is sacramental, and it is through our flesh that we receive the grace of Christ.

Jesus Christ gave us the seven sacraments for a similar reason. They are "efficacious signs of grace, instituted by Christ and entrusted to the Church, by which divine life is dispensed to us" (CCC 1131). They are visible signs of invisible realities. As the water of Baptism is more than just a cleansing liquid, and the bread and wine offered in the Eucharist are more than just physical food, the body is more than just matter. The body, like the symbols associated with the sacraments of Baptism and the Eucharist, is life-giving. The waters of Baptism really do wash away sin. They really are life-giving, filling us with the graces needed for eternal life in heaven. And the bread and wine really are changed into Jesus' Body and Blood in the Eucharist. The Eucharist is life-giving, and it really is the bread and wine that are changed in transubstantiation so that we can receive Jesus' Body and Blood, which give us eternal life. Something similar can be said for the body: "It is because of its spiritual soul that the body made of matter becomes a living, human body" (CCC 365).

If the body is the sacrament of the soul, that means we don't really *have* bodies. Being a body is essential to being human; in fact, it's as essential as being a soul. Neither is fully human. Every human person is a united body and soul. We are ensouled bodies, or better yet, embodied souls. The body is the sacrament of the soul, the physical sign pointing to the spiritual, invisible reality. But the body is just as essential to us as water is to Baptism, or bread and wine is to the Eucharist. We can't be truly human without our bodies.

REDISCOVERING THE SACRAMENT

Adam and Eve experienced the proper relationship between the body and soul, a union that was only possible before the Fall. We can visualize this communion but only as outsiders, since we cannot live apart from the effects of sin. We can do our best to imagine this pre-fallen world using the words of Scripture and our imaginations, and what we know of it can give us hope for the future. We know what we were created for. We know what God planned for us. And we know that God is not done with us yet.

We are not meant to be at war with our bodies. They are not some evil source of temptation, a curse that pulls us away from union with God. When God created us, he made us to be embodied souls. Our bodies were meant to reveal our souls, to show the world what lies within us. Our bodies and souls are meant to be united, to work together for the glory of God. I am my body just as much as I am my soul. When we consider our bodies as something outside of ourselves, something we can control and manipulate as meaningless matter, we are living a lie. Our bodies do matter, and they could never truly be meaningless.

If we are at war with our bodies, it is because humanity is fallen and we are inclined to sin. When Adam and Eve ate the forbidden fruit, they broke the original communion they had once experienced. That is why we find ourselves at war with ourselves, with each other, with the world, and even with God (though that one is a one-sided war). We are not the enemy. Our bodies are not the enemy. God is certainly not the enemy.

Fighting sin and Satan is the war that we are called to wage, and it will not be won by making our bodies the enemy. As St. John Paul II writes, referring to St. Paul's letter to the Galatians,

> for the Apostle, it is not a matter of despising and condemning the body with which the spiritual soul constitutes man's nature ... Rather, he is concerned with the morally *good* or *bad* works, or better, the permanent dispositions—virtues and vices—which are the fruit of submission (in the first case) or of *resistance* (in the second case) to the *saving action of the Holy Spirit.* For this reason the Apostle writes: "If we live by the Spirit, let us also walk by the Spirit."[4]

Once we've identified the true enemy, we can be better prepared to fight the war. We are at war, and it's a fight we will continue to wage until the day we die. But it's not a war against our bodies. It's a war for our souls. Whenever we are tempted to degrade our bodies, we must choose to love them instead. Whenever we hear the message that we are too big, or too small, or too whatever, we have to remind ourselves that those are all lies from the pit of hell, and God has a different message for us. God tells us, "You are all fair, my love; there is no flaw in you" (Song of Solomon 4:7).

---

4   John Paul II, *Dominum et Vivificantem* 55; see also Galatians 5:25. *Quoted in CCC 2516.*

And then we are encouraged to respond with the Psalmist, "I praise you, for I am wondrously made. Wonderful are your works!" (Psalm 139:14).

Our bodies were only ever meant to be a sacrament, a place where grace was meant to dwell, the dwelling place of the Holy Spirit himself. They were meant to be man's way of communicating himself to the world and, more specifically, to other human persons. And it is by living among other human persons that we can rediscover our bodies as the sacraments they are.

WINNING THE WAR THROUGH SURRENDER

The war I waged against my body did not end until I became pregnant with my first child. Faced with the reality that my poor decisions were now hurting someone other than myself, I was finally forced to admit that my decisions were harmful. Now when I starved myself, I was starving my baby. When I punished myself by running extra miles, I was punishing my baby. And if I was hurting my baby with my choices, I had to admit that my choices were hurting me as well. So I started forming healthy habits, making choices that respected the dignity of my body and honored its needs. Whenever I was faced with a decision about food or exercise, I had to make it with my baby in mind, and because of the selflessness demanded by motherhood, I began to heal.

After the birth of my son, I continued to make good choices. Over nine months, I had developed the good habits necessary to be healthy, and I liked the way I felt. I liked the way my body felt. And after nine months of pregnancy and twelve hours of labor, I was proud of my body. I was proud of what it had done, sustaining the life of a healthy baby boy and then bringing that child into the world. I was proud of what it was still doing on a daily basis to care for my son. My arms were strong from carrying my child, and my legs were robust from bouncing him. I was healthy enough to chase after my son when he began to run, and I had enough energy to play with him on the playground. I was healthy and happy, and I could finally see that my body was not the enemy, and never had been.

Making good choices has been difficult at times, but knowing that I am choosing to love God, my children, and myself through those choices has made them easier to make. I struggle sometimes, but my children give me the perspective I need to persevere, to get up when I fall down, to keep pushing even when I want to throw in the towel. When I was pregnant with my son, I knew that I couldn't keep up the war against my body without him becoming a casualty, so I surrendered. But in surrendering, I realized that I was the one waging the war, not my body, and it had always been within my power to end it. And by surrendering, I was victorious.

Rather than trying to suffer and overcome our struggles alone, we can surrender them to God and unite them to the cross of Christ. By surrendering, we can win battles in the only war worth fighting—the war against sin and the Devil. It's a war we will all continue to fight until the day we die, when we hope to claim the greatest, and final, victory—heaven. And I know that's a war worth fighting.

QUESTIONS FOR REFLECTION

1. What are some of your favorite physical characteristics about your body? Why?

2. Why could Adam and Eve be naked and unashamed?

3. What are some times in your life when you have felt proud of your body?

4. How was mankind meant to experience communion—with God, with the world, with the sexes, and within himself?

5. What are the dangers in treating our bodies as something external to us, as matter to be manipulated and shaped? What are the dangers in treating our bodies like the enemy?

An Exercise in Seeing Yourself as God Does

GOD'S VIEW OF HIS CREATION

In this chapter, we saw how our bodies were meant to reveal our souls, to show the world what lies within us. When we are consumed with shame about our bodies, we forget their goodness and purpose. Shame is an emotion that can urge us to hide from ourselves, from others, and from God. When hiding in shame and detached from the true purpose of our bodies, we can begin to despair. Instead of continuing to be ruled by shame, consider bringing your pain and discomfort to the One who made you, using the following exercise.

1. Get a pen and several pieces of paper and find a quiet space to spend some time alone.

2. Write a letter to the Lord about your struggle with your body. Allow yourself to speak freely about what you think and feel. Consider sharing with God the timeline of your struggle. How does your struggle affect your relationships? Your faith? Nothing is too big or small to bring to the Lord.

3. You may need to stop and take a break. That's OK! Be gentle with yourself during this exercise. You may find the

urge to hide away parts of your experience. Try to allow uncomfortable emotions to be present while choosing to reveal yourself to the Lord.

4. After you have completed your letter to the Lord, you may need some time to process this experience. When you are ready, whether that is after a few minutes, a few hours, or a few days, return to your pen and paper.

5. Knowing that God made your body to reveal your soul and that you are his handiwork, write the letter you think the Lord might send to you. How does he see his creation? What aspects of your soul are revealed through your body? How have you used your body for his glory?

6. Continue to notice the thoughts and feelings that arise during this exercise. It can be hard to hear gentle and compassionate words when we are mired in shame. Just try to note your experience without judgment.

7. When you have finished this exercise, consider how your perception of your body is similar to or different from how our Lord may see you. What might he see that is hard for you to see?

8. Continue to bring your struggle to the Lord. Allow him to speak into your shame and struggle.

3

Motherhood and the Body

Motherhood completely revolutionized the way that I looked at my body. Whereas I once spent time every morning cataloging my body's flaws, now I spend time every morning marveling at what my body has done. The human body is capable of so many incredible things, and the female body in particular is extraordinary in its capabilities. A miracle happens within the female body every time a child is conceived. Life exists where it once did not. What were once just two cells have become one human being, one embodied soul. God creates a human person with our cooperation, joining our flesh and blood with his divine life. The love shared between a husband and wife does not have the power to give life without the life-giving breath of God. We give our children their bodies, but it is God who bestows upon them their souls. And that extraordinary miracle happens within the body of woman. Our bodies. Our beautiful, God-given bodies.

When I was growing up, I didn't think that my body was beautiful, so I endlessly criticized it, punished it, and hid it away. That completely changed while I was pregnant. I loved my body. I loved watching the bump on my abdomen grow as the baby grew within me. I loved stroking my round stomach, knowing that when the world saw me, they saw a pregnant woman. They could not judge me for my weight. They could not judge me for the amount of food I ate at dinner. They could not judge me for the way I struggled to move around quickly and comfortably. I was pregnant, and I felt invulnerable.

That sense of invulnerability actually survived the births of both of my children, at least for a time. A week after my daughter was born, I remember taking my two kids for a walk one afternoon and feeling absolutely incredible. I felt shockingly comfortable in my own skin, despite the fact that I was still wearing maternity workout clothes. My body looked nothing like it had pre-pregnancy, but I didn't care. I was too overwhelmingly proud of what my body had done. Nothing could make me feel differently about my amazing body—nothing but the passing of time and my own fallen nature.

Months later, as I was scrolling through my photo gallery on my phone, I stumbled across a picture my mother-in-law had taken of the kids and me on that day during our walk. I could still remember how I had felt that day, how comfortable I had felt in my own skin, and how happy I had been with my life as a new mother of two. I had a very strong memory of those feelings, but as I stared at the photo, all I could see was how round my stomach was, how soft it looked framed in that maternity top. I took in all the details, and I cringed. I might have felt beautiful when that photo was taken, but as I stared at the picture, all I could think was, *I definitely don't look beautiful.*

As the months passed and I became further and further removed from the day I gave birth to my daughter, the temptation to critique my body resurfaced. Despite the fact that I had returned to "normal," I felt that my "flaws" were many—stretch marks, wider hips, and a softness I did not possess before. My body did not look the way that it had before becoming pregnant, and I was reluctant to embrace these changes. The temptation to hide my body was strong, and in this era of athleisure-wear and loose-fitting tunics, it's been easy to hide the evidence of my childbearing from the world. But in those moments when I am tempted to catalog my faults, I instead choose to focus on my body's accomplishments. The flaws become a badge of honor, proof that I have carried a miracle, two miracles in fact, within me. And when you have been touched by the divine, when you have been filled with the miraculous, you can't help but be proud.

ESSENTIAL MOTHERHOOD

Motherhood is an essential part of being female. Not every woman will give birth to a child, but all women are mothers in some way. We are all born with that inherent ability to offer comfort, that natural desire to care for others. Even before I was married, when I was working as a religious educator and youth minister, I was a mother to the children I taught. Even earlier than that, I witnessed countless religious sisters who treated the girls in my high school as if they were their own daughters, and in some cases, these unmarried, childless women were more motherly to those girls than their own mothers were to them. I knew by the time I was fourteen that you didn't need to have biological children to be a mother.

In modern culture, we are so reluctant to highlight those characteristics that make us uniquely feminine, that separate us from men. We are trying to push for female equality, which is commendable, but by associating equality with sameness, we are doing all women a huge disservice. We are ignoring all the beautiful qualities that make us unique as women. We are ignoring the characteristics that allow women to excel in their roles as mothers, whether they have biological children or not.

There is a reason that the first account of creation tells us, "In the image of God he created him; male and female he created them" (Genesis 1:27). The image of God goes beyond our abilities to think and choose; our very existence as men and women is part of that divine imaging. God might only ever be called "Father," and for good reason, but even the Scriptures use motherhood as a common metaphor for God.

> *You forgot the God who gave you birth. (Deuteronomy 32:18)*
>
> *As one whom his mother comforts, so I will comfort you. (Isaiah 66:13)*
>
> *Can a woman forget her sucking child, that she should have no compassion on the son of her womb? Even these may forget, yet I will not forget you. (Isaiah 49:15)*

God is our Father, and as the Scriptures here say, he loves us like a mother. He created us, giving us form in his mind as he gave us life on this earth. He offers us comfort, just as a mother comforts her child. And just as a mother could never forget her child, the fruit of her womb, God could never forget any of us, the fruit of his divine love. And what's more? God does a better job revealing the truths of motherhood than we ever could, even those of us who are physically mothers ourselves. He possesses the qualities of motherhood in their fullness; we possess them as a reflection of God.

Motherhood allows us to be like God. We are able to co-create with him, bringing new life into this world after having carried it within us. We love our children as only mothers can, comforting them and always carrying them in the forefront of our minds. We suffer when we see our children suffer, mourn when they become lost, and rejoice when they find their way home again. We are able to be mothers ourselves because God first showed us the essence of motherhood in his love for us.

Men and women image God in a unique way, and together we paint a fuller picture of who God is. Men are a reflection of how God provides for and protects us. God not only created us; he also provides for all of our needs. He gives us "our daily bread," the physical and spiritual sustenance we need to survive and thrive. God also protects us, delivering us from evil and leading us along the path to eternal life. Man's ability to protect and provide for his family is at the core of his masculinity. The traits that make a man a good father are precisely those that make him a good man.

Women, on the other hand, are a reflection of how God nurtures and supports us. Again, God didn't just create us and leave us to do our own thing. He sustains us. He holds us in existence. He nurtures us with his life and his Word, refreshing our souls. He teaches us so that we might grow "in wisdom and in stature, and in favor with God and man" (Luke 2:52). He comforts us in our afflictions, rejoices with us in our triumphs, and mourns with us in our sorrows. Woman's ability to nurture and support her family is at the core of her femininity. Again, the traits that make a woman a good mother are what make her a good woman.

Fatherhood and motherhood are at the core of our identity as male and female. They are essential to our masculinity and femininity. That means that all men are called to fatherhood in some way, and all women are called to motherhood in some way. Not all men and women become biological parents, but we are all called to be mothers and fathers. We are called to live out our masculinity and femininity as images of God in the world. Fatherhood and motherhood are often biological and physical, but they are also spiritual.

All women are changed by their vocation to be mothers, whether it is a physical or spiritual calling. When we give up our bodies for those we love, we are irrevocably changed. When we endure sleepless nights agonizing over our children, we are changed. When we stress over the futures of our students, we are changed. When we gain weight while giving life to our unborn children, we are changed. We might be able to see the rounded bellies and hips, or the bags under our eyes, or the wrinkles on our faces, but the changes are not just physical. They touch us at our very core. When we answer the call to become mothers, we become more fully the women that God is calling us to be—curves, bags, and all. We become the beautiful masterpieces God had planned from before our births.

MOTHERHOOD AND THE IMAGE OF GOD

When God created woman, he already had motherhood in mind. Before the first pregnancy, before the first conception of a child in the womb of his mother, God envisioned motherhood for his beloved daughters. Being outside of time himself, God held in his divine mind the lives of Cain and Abel, of Seth and all those children who came after him, every child who would emerge from the womb of Eve, who was "the mother of all living" (Genesis 3:20). He held in his mind the new Eve, the Virgin Mary, who would be born of the womb of Anne, who would go on to be the mother of Life himself, Jesus Christ. Before any of these women became mothers themselves, God held in his mind the children that they would bear. These women had been born to be mothers.

Motherhood had always been part of God's plan for mankind, but we can only speculate about what pregnancy and childbirth might have looked like in an unfallen world. As Scripture tells us, Adam and Eve did not conceive a child until after they had sinned. They committed the first sin before their love could bear fruit in the form of a child. But we do know that motherhood had always been part of God's plan for his masterpiece. If we image God in our capacities as mothers and fathers, motherhood and fatherhood were both part of the plan from the beginning. Man and woman's ability to bring life into this world, to give life to their very love in the form of children, is one of the ways that man reflects God. Our vocation to be mothers and fathers is part of the image of God within us. Motherhood and fatherhood reveal something of God to the world.

The communion of persons has traditionally been used as a metaphor for the Trinity, and John Paul II affirms this when he writes,

> Man became the image of God not only through his own humanity, but also through the communion of persons ... He is, in fact, "from the beginning" not only an image in which the solitude of one Person, who rules the world, mirrors itself, but also and essentially the image of an inscrutable divine communion of Persons. (TOB 9.3)

God is a communion of persons, and since we are made in the image of God, we are called to communion as well. We live out this communion in our vocations, one of which is the call to holy marriage.

Man and woman are called to image God in a very beautiful way, unique to their circumstances. Their marital love is meant to be a reflection of divine love, which by nature is total, free, faithful, and fruitful. This is what we promise when we exchange marriage vows. We give ourselves to the other freely, for all time, faithfully, and fruitfully, and sometimes that fruitfulness takes the form of another person, a child. Our love is meant to be a reflection of the love that exists between the Persons of the Blessed Trinity. The Father and Son love each other so much that the fruit of their love is a distinct person, the Holy Spirit. Their bond of love is so overabundant that it is life-giving. When we reflect the love of God, we are the image of the Trinity made present to the whole world. How awesome is that?

God created men and women in his image. His image is going to be communal because he himself is a Trinity. God is three Persons in one divine Godhead. God is love. God is a communion of Persons. Since we are made in the image of this Trinitarian God, we are called to love and to give ourselves to others in love and to live in communion with those other people. We are made to love and be loved, and that love has the capacity to beget another person, the fruit of that love, a child. Like the love of the Father and Son begets a third Person, the Holy Spirit, the love of husband and wife has the potential to give birth to another life, their child. And women experience this reality in a unique and powerful way, since we have that love come to life within us.

THE MIRACLE OF PREGNANCY

Every time a woman becomes pregnant, her body holds a miracle within it. Matter takes form. Cells are ensouled. Life is created where there was no life before. Pregnancy might be common, but its regularity makes it no less miraculous. We can't conceive on our own, after all. Only God can give life. We are witnesses to the miracle, participants even, but life is a miracle that lies outside of our human abilities.

It was always part of God's plan for women that we be witnesses to the miracle of life, that we be able to carry the miracle within us and bring that miracle into the world. Eve might not have become pregnant prior to the Fall, but it's clear that God always intended that Eve be a mother. Pregnancy was not a consequence of the Fall; difficult childbirth was. We were always meant to bring children into the world, but now we must do so with pain and suffering.

The marks of motherhood are not all the result of the Fall, though. Sure, the scars that come from tearing during childbirth or from a C-section can properly be called a consequence of the Fall, but many of the other "scars," which we might consider flaws, are actually marks of the miracle of motherhood. They should be badges of honor for all women rather than sources of shame.

When our bodies and hearts stretch to accommodate the growth of a new life within us, it leaves a mark. When our bodies shift and reshape themselves to grant a child safe passage to this new world, it leaves a mark. When our bodies provide comfort and nourishment to that child, it leaves a mark. By the time my son turned one, I still didn't look the same. My hips remained perpetually wider, my stomach maintained just a bit more softness than it had before, and my hair never returned to being stick straight. These marks are not bad; they just make my body look and feel different. But four years after the birth of my second child, I've come to accept that these wider hips, soft abdomen, and curly locks are my new normal. They are mine to keep, my own personal marks of motherhood.

Motherhood will always leave its mark, just as any life-changing experience will. Our bodies do not want us to forget what we have done in the name of love. Our bodies do not want us to forget the miracles that we have held within us. We should be proud of those bodies, proud of ourselves, and proud of the marks that we bear that bear witness to our motherhood. They are all part of the masterpiece that God is creating with my life, and they are beautiful.

SPIRITUAL MOTHERHOOD

Motherhood is a natural outpouring of our femininity. We are all called to be mothers, whether that means bringing our own children into the world and raising them, adopting or fostering children that belong to our hearts but were never part of our bodies, or loving children who are not ours and have their own parents but are still linked to us by love. For all of us, motherhood will have a spiritual dimension. Motherhood goes beyond just our physical ability to become pregnant and give birth. Teachers are mothers to their students. Aunts are mothers to their nieces and nephews. Older sisters are mothers to their younger siblings. Religious sisters are mothers to everyone. All women are mothers in some way.

At the core of who we are as women, we find our ability to *mother*. That feminine intuition, that strong need to provide comfort and security, that instinct that leads us to consider another's emotions and needs before our own—these are all evidence of the innate vocation to spiritual motherhood. Even my daughter, who is only four, exhibits this need to mother. While her older brother lines up his toys (as well as some of her dolls) so that they might do battle against each other, my daughter will spend hours caring for her toys. They are repeatedly dressed, fed, burped, put down for naps, and snuggled. Her dolls all have emotions—she has on more than one occasion informed me that "Ballerina Bitty" is sad because she needs a hug—and my daughter is always looking for ways to comfort and care for her dolls. For as long as she has been playing with her dolls, my daughter has been a mother to them.

For some of us, our call to motherhood will be lived out physically, but not all of us will experience the joys and sorrows of pregnancy and childbirth. Some of us will choose to forgo pregnancy and childbirth to become brides of Christ and spiritual mothers as religious sisters or nuns. Others will choose to adopt or foster children, becoming physical mothers by embracing their spiritual motherhood. And still others will remain childless through no choice of their own, but they will still be able to choose to be spiritual mothers to the people in their lives through their family relationships, jobs, and friendships. No matter how we live out our motherhood, we are all called to be mothers. It is essential to our femininity.

This has been evident to me since I was a teenager. I attended an all-girls Catholic high school that was adjacent to a convent housing roughly twenty-five religious sisters (affectionately called "nuns" from here on out, although this term is incorrect since they were not cloistered religious). I had a nun for a principal. One nun taught gymnastics classes, and another coached volleyball. My precalculus teacher was a nun. They were everywhere. They taught us, ate with us, played with us. If you've never seen a nun shoot a three-pointer in basketball (and score), or spike a volleyball with such ferocity that her opponents cower in fear, it's quite the sight to see. They offered us their prayers, their time, and their lives. They mothered us in ways that some of our own mothers could not (because even the best-behaved teenage girl still needs a female confidant who is not her mother), and I know of more than one girl who considered one of the nuns to be more of a mom to her than her own mother. Those nuns loved us. They might not have given birth to us, or even raised us as children, but those women truly loved us as mothers. They were undeniably women living out their feminine vocation to motherhood, and they are powerful reminders that while not all women will become pregnant and give birth, they have all been born to be mothers.

Religious sisters, aunts, godmothers, and teachers are all wonderful reminders that motherhood is not purely physical. Even for us biological mothers, motherhood extends beyond our ability to bear children. We are also tasked with educating our children and raising them in the Faith to become upstanding citizens and virtuous Christians. But we are not alone in this responsibility. As the saying goes, it takes a village to raise a child. As a child, my primary caregiver was my mom, but aunts, older cousins, friends' moms, and my teachers all played a role in my education and maturation. Similarly, I might be my kids' mom, but I am eternally grateful to the other women in my life who are helping me to raise my children. All the women in my life have answered their call in amazing ways, and they are all wonderful testaments to the power of spiritual motherhood.

THE VIRGIN MOTHER MARY

Motherhood is so important in the mind of God that he used it as the means to our redemption. Our Savior, God himself, became man by first residing in the body of a woman. God received his human flesh and blood from a woman. God nursed at the breasts of a woman, was held in the arms of a woman, and was cared for and raised to maturity by a woman. Jesus Christ is the Son of God, but he is also the son of Mary, his mother.

Mary is proof that pregnancy and motherhood were intended to be part of God's plan for woman, even before the Fall.[5] Mary, preserved from sin and immaculately conceived, became the mother of Jesus by first carrying him in her womb. Her flesh stretched to accommodate his growing body. Her body shifted and reshaped itself so that her Son could be ushered into this world. Her breasts filled with milk to nourish the Son of God. Mary became pregnant, and her body experienced all the appropriate physical signs of pregnancy.

Though Christ was conceived through the power of the Holy Spirit and Mary was a virgin before, during, and after the birth of her Son, for nine months she truly was pregnant and carried her child within her womb. Though Mary experienced none of the pains of childbirth, she still gave birth to her child on that monumental night in Bethlehem. Her experiences of pregnancy and childbirth were unique (and radically so), but they were still that—experiences of pregnancy and childbirth.

Mary bore many of the marks of motherhood in her body, just as any woman who has become pregnant does. Her womb expanded as her baby boy grew, and her skin stretched and became taut as well. Her flesh, though perfect and preserved from the effects of sin, still bore the natural effects of pregnancy. She would have gained weight during her pregnancy, providing her son with the nutrients that he needed to grow and thrive. Her breasts would have swelled in preparation to nurse her infant son. Mary experienced all the physical consequences of pregnancy and postpartum life. These are just the natural marks of motherhood,

---

5   God intended for women to be able to conceive and bear children, but because of the Fall and our existence in a fallen world, not all women can conceive children themselves. Infertility is a very real struggle faced by many women, a heavy cross that more than one in ten women find themselves carrying, according to a World Health Organization report.

and the Mother of God would certainly have carried them as well. But she would have carried them as a badge of honor, in gratitude to God for his wonderful works, and not as flaws that needed to be hidden. Jesus Christ presents his mother as the perfect role model for motherhood, and we are invited to carry that badge of honor too, just like Mary did.

BEARING THE MARKS OF MOTHERHOOD WITH GRACE

I'll be honest—I spent way too much time debating whether or not Mary had stretch marks in preparation for writing this chapter. In fact, I spent days agonizing over that single question. While certain characteristics of pregnancy and childbirth, like contraction pains and tearing, are obviously consequences of the Fall, other marks are more complicated. How much of our experience of pregnancy and childbirth is the result of the fall of man, and how much of it is simply appropriate to motherhood? Mary is the answer to that question. She experienced pregnancy and childbirth as God intended all women to experience it prior to the Fall, but unfortunately for us, the Gospels do not include a detailed account of Mary's experience. There are no clear answers.

After days of agonizing over the theological implications of my theories, I realized something. I didn't need a clear answer, not where my own healing was concerned, anyway. Mary might have had stretch marks; her body might have changed shape after the birth of her son. She might have had wider hips after giving birth; she might have felt the heaviness of breasts filled with milk. She might have, and she might not have. In the end, it doesn't matter for me. The fact that I was so focused on the answers to those questions was just proof that I was still too focused on my apparent "flaws."

If Mary had stretch marks, she didn't count them. If she had wider hips, she didn't measure them. If her body looked different after the birth of Jesus, she didn't dwell on it. If Mary bore any of those physical marks of pregnancy and childbirth, she would not have viewed them as flaws—because they couldn't have been flaws, not for her. Mary is perfect. So if she carried them, those marks did not mar her perfection. Even with them, she remained immaculate.

Mary was perfect in mind and body. If she possessed any of those marks of pregnancy that I consider flaws, Mary would not have berated herself for them. She would have embraced them. She would have been grateful for them because they were reminders of the incredible miracle she had carried within her. Mary would not have been afflicted by the weakness of the fallen human person. She would have seen her marks as nothing other than what they were—marks of her motherhood. Not scars, but a symbol of her love. Not flaws, but badges of honor. Not something to hide, but something to celebrate and embrace.

I am not Mary. I am not perfect, and my imperfect brain is going to see imperfections that don't exist. The Devil is going to whisper into my fallen mind that these marks of my motherhood, my femininity, are flaws. They are things I need to hide, things I should be ashamed of. But that's just the Father of Lies talking. And he's just jealous. He hates us because our marks of motherhood are a constant reminder of his epic defeat through a woman. God used a woman, a mother, to defeat Satan. A woman brought God himself into the world and held him in her womb before she held his body at the foot of the cross. The cross is a reminder of how the Devil's defeat ended, but the pregnant woman is where it all began.

No wonder Satan wants us to believe the lies so badly. He wants us to be ashamed of our crowning achievement because it is a reminder of his utter defeat. But we shouldn't be ashamed. We shouldn't listen to Satan's lies. Instead, we should listen to the whispers of God in our hearts. Motherhood was always part of God's plan for us. It is essential to who we are as women. Motherhood is a gift from God, an opportunity for mankind to cooperate with God and to add our own flesh and blood to the life he breathes into our children. And after our bodies have been touched by such an incredible miracle, it should come as no surprise that our bodies will never be quite the same again.

QUESTIONS FOR REFLECTION

1. What are some characteristics that are unique to women? How do these traits relate to the fact that women are made in the image of God?

2. Why do you think the Scriptures use metaphors of motherhood to describe God's relationship with the world?

3. What are some ways that families reflect the Trinity in their daily lives?

4. What are some of the ways that you have lived out your call to motherhood?

5. How is Mary the perfect role model for all women and mothers?

An Exercise in Seeing Yourself as God Does

COMPASSION REMINDERS

When painful thoughts and feelings are present, it can be easy to become tangled in them and fall into unhelpful ways of coping with them. Consider placing small cues around your home to help remind you to take stock of your current feelings, turn your eyes to God, and engage your suffering with compassion and kindness. Here are some examples:

- If you struggle when looking in the mirror in the morning, tape a picture of the Blessed Mother on the mirror to remind you to shift your attention from difficult thoughts and feelings back out to the world around you.

- Find some quotes from your favorite saints to remind you how to live and suffer well. For example, the writings of St. Francis de Sales are full of wisdom about peace and compassion in suffering! Then, place them around your home. This can be as simple as writing the quotes on sticky notes and sticking them to surfaces you pass frequently (the fridge, the steering wheel, your bathroom mirror, the back of your phone, or inside your wallet). You could also print them out or, if you're crafty, design them yourself.

Part 2
· · · · · · · · ·
YOU ARE BROKEN

4

The Fall of Man

Junior year was the year of what I call my "reversion"—my return to practicing the Catholic Faith. It was 2006, and I had begun that year as a borderline agnostic who just didn't really care about the Faith. But after a weekend-long youth conference that completely changed the way I viewed God, I ended the year as a young woman who was in love with the Lord.

Junior year was also the year of the now infamous (at least in my mind) comment by my classmate criticizing my appearance. Just as I began to really adopt the Catholic Faith as my own, I also began my decade-long battle with body image issues and an eating disorder. Just as I began to get my faith life in order, my self-esteem and mental health began to crumble.

Fast-forward three years. It was 2009, and I was majoring in theology in college, with dreams of eventually teaching or working in youth ministry. I spent my weekends and school breaks leading retreats, and I even helped to create a few from scratch. I was heavily involved in our campus ministry programs and attended Mass nearly every day of the week. To say that I was in love with God and my Catholic Faith would be an understatement.

At the same time, I began restricting calories, over-exercising, and researching other weight-loss methods. I worked hard to hide my secrets from my roommate so that she wouldn't suspect what I was doing. I was obsessed with lowering the number on the scale using whatever means was necessary. I was slowly losing control and was desperately trying to get it back. To say that I was sick would be an understatement, but I didn't realize it back then.

Fast-forward another three years. It was the spring of 2012, and I had just left my master's program, where I had been pursuing another degree in theology, in order to discern a possible religious vocation. While in formation, I spent my days praying, studying, and assisting at our order's local high school. My prayer life was intense and invigorating, and when I prayed, I couldn't imagine feeling any closer to God. But that feeling didn't extend beyond the chapel.

In my bedroom at night, I felt alone and abandoned. I was sneaking around the convent at night, binging and purging while the sisters slept, and over-exercising whenever I thought I could hide my actions. I couldn't understand how I could feel so close to God but also feel so alone.

For years, I couldn't understand why my faith didn't seem to have any effect on my mental health. Was I not praying hard enough? Was my faith not strong enough? I worried about what people might think or say if they found out that despite my seemingly solid faith, I still struggled with intense body image issues and an eating disorder. Would they doubt my faith? Would they doubt the power of my prayer?

After a decade of struggling to understand the relationship between my faith and my mental health, I finally realized the truth. God might always have the answer, but that answer will often go beyond just simple prayer. We are not just spiritual souls, and my problem was not just spiritual. We have bodies too, and our brains are usually not cured through prayer alone. The fall of man had both spiritual and physical consequences, punishments that were appropriate for a creature that was an embodied soul. As a result, our healing must be both spiritual and physical.

THE ORIGINAL SIN OF ADAM AND EVE

Now the serpent was more subtle than any other wild creature that the LORD God had made. He said to the woman, "Did God say, 'You shall not eat of any tree of the garden'?" And the woman said to the serpent, "We may eat of the fruit of the trees of the garden; but God said, 'You shall not eat of the fruit of the tree which is in the midst of the garden, neither shall you touch it, lest you die.'" But the serpent said to the woman, "You will not die. For God knows that when you eat of it your eyes will be opened, and you will be like God, knowing good and evil." So when the woman saw that the tree was good for food, and that it was a delight to the eyes, and that the tree was to be desired to make one wise, she took of its fruit and ate; and she also gave some to her husband, and he ate.

[God said,] "Have you eaten of the tree of which I commanded you not to eat?" The man said, "The woman whom you gave to be with me, she gave me fruit of the tree, and I ate." Then the LORD God said to the woman, "What is this that you have

done?" The woman said, "The serpent beguiled me, and I ate."

The LORD God said to the serpent, "Because you have done this, cursed are you above all cattle, and above all wild animals; upon your belly you shall go, and dust you shall eat all the days of your life. I will put enmity between you and the woman, and between your seed and her seed; he shall bruise your head, and you shall bruise his heel."

To the woman he said, "I will greatly multiply your pain in childbearing; in pain you shall bring forth children, yet your desire shall be for your husband, and he shall rule over you."

And to Adam he said, "Because you have listened to the voice of your wife, and have eaten of the tree of which I commanded you, 'You shall not eat of it,' cursed is the ground because of you; in toil you shall eat of it all the days of your life; thorns and thistles it shall bring forth to you; and you shall eat the plants of the field. In the sweat of your face you shall eat bread till you return to the ground, for out of it you were taken; you are dust, and to dust you shall return." (Genesis 3:1-6, 3:11-19)

So what was that original sin of Adam and Eve, really? In all my years studying the Faith, I have heard many answers—pride, envy, lust, a lack of trust in God. In truth, I can see how all of these sins might have reared their ugly heads at that first disobedience. Adam and Eve were too proud to play second fiddle to God. They were jealous of his divinity and wanted it for themselves. They lusted after that fruit of temptation, the desire to treat other people as objects for their own pleasure. They did not trust that God had their best interests in mind when he told them not to eat of the fruit of the tree in the middle of the Garden. All of these explanations seem to be connected.

Adam and Eve did not just want to be "like God." They wanted to be God. They were already like God, just as they were—they had been created in his image and likeness, after all. God wanted Adam and Eve to be like him; that had always been part of his plan for mankind. Adam and Eve just weren't willing to wait. God had the final masterpiece in mind, but Adam and Eve were content with the rough draft. They got impatient, and they doomed all mankind because of it.

Adam and Eve wanted to be gods themselves. They rejected their creature status since it was a constant reminder they were not God. Adam and Eve wrongly assumed that if they ate the fruit, they could take that divinity for themselves. They didn't want to have it given to them; they wanted to take it. They wanted divinity on their own terms.

The greatest irony of that original sin? Adam and Eve were grasping for something that God had always intended to give them. God had always planned to allow mankind to partake in his divinity. If they had been a bit more patient, if they had spent a bit more time walking with God in the Garden of Eden, maybe they would have realized their mistake. Adam and Eve just didn't understand their God. And they didn't understand themselves fully either. Hence the Fall.

As fallen creatures, we can all share in that misunderstanding. We all have a "definition" of God, but even the most accurate description of him is going to be paltry compared to the full reality. God is so much more than what our human minds can comprehend. He is infinite, and we are finite. We will *never* fully understand God because there will always be more to know. And this is all assuming that what we do believe about God is right. God has revealed himself to us in countless ways, but we are all sometimes tempted to define him according to our terms. We claim that God cannot love us because we're too much or not enough. We believe that he demands a physical perfection that is just impossible for us. We assume that his love is dependent on our abilities or our appearances. But that is just not how God has revealed himself to us. That is not who God is.

ENTERTAINING THE FATHER OF LIES

Satan is cunning. When he tempted Adam and Eve to consume the fruit they had been forbidden to eat, he promised that they would receive the very thing they longed for: equality with God. But unlike Jesus Christ, who received his divinity from the Father, Adam and Eve were not satisfied to have their divinity given to them. They desired to take it, to steal it and claim it as theirs. So the Serpent tempted them, saying, "You will not die. For God knows that when you eat of it your eyes will be opened, and you will be like God, knowing good and evil" (Genesis 3:4–5).

Satan told Adam and Eve exactly what they wanted to hear. It didn't matter that it wasn't true. Satan promised that the fruit would give them exactly what they wanted, and there the fruit was, ripe for the taking. For stealing. For usurping. It didn't matter that God said they would die. Adam and Eve didn't trust him. They believed that God was hiding things from them, purposely keeping them in the dark. They assumed that by eating the fruit, they would finally be able to truly see. They would know good and evil. More specifically, they would be able to determine what was good and evil for themselves. They would be little gods, and with no help from God in achieving it. Adam and Eve thought they could do it all by themselves.

Adam and Eve were deathly wrong. The fruit did bring death. Determining good and evil was not all it was cracked up to be. But by then it was too late to go back. So Adam and Eve did the only thing they could do; they hid. As if God wouldn't be able to find them. As if he didn't already know what they had done. As if they could keep their secret from his all-seeing eyes. But they were wrong, and they paid for their sin with their lives, and the lives of every one of their children, through all generations until the coming of Christ.

We all hide from God from time to time. We, like Adam and Eve, believe that if we hide well enough, he won't find us. We believe that we can hide our shame the same way that we hide our supposed disfigurements, scars, and imperfections. But baggy clothes and thick makeup can't hide us from our God. As the psalmist says,

> Where shall I go from your Spirit?
>> Or where shall I flee from your presence?
> If I ascend to heaven, you are there!
>> If I make my bed in Sheol, you are there!
> If I take the wings of the morning
>> and dwell in the uttermost parts of the sea,
> even there your hand shall lead me,
>> and your right hand shall hold me.
>>> (Psalm 139:7-10)

We all eventually learn that there is no place that we can hide from God.

Not that we really want to hide from him. Even Adam and Eve did not wait long before revealing themselves. They were ashamed of their behavior, but the need to be close to God overrode their shame. We all want to be found. We play hide-and-seek the same way my kids do—badly. My daughter likes to sit in her hiding spot with her feet sticking out, and my son will start coughing and laughing if I leave him alone too long. They hide, but they desperately want to be found. And so do we. We try so hard to hide—from God, from our family, from our spouses and children—but we also want to be *seen*. We want our loved ones to see us as we are and love us anyway. We just need to learn to see ourselves the way God sees us, as the beautiful works of art we are. Maybe then we would finally stop hiding.

THE TWO-FOLD CURSE OF DEATH

The punishments for Adam and Eve's sin were many. Both man and woman were punished individually, affected by consequences that struck who they were at their very core. Man would struggle against the earth to provide food for his family, and woman would suffer in childbirth. But mankind was also collectively punished. As God had warned, eating the fruit brought death, and not just physical death but spiritual death as well.

Adam and Eve had been given two forms of life at their creation: *bios*, or physical life, and *zoe*, spiritual life. The first they shared with all other living creatures; the second they shared only with God, who had given it to them. The fall of man brought death to both forms of life. After eating the fruit, Adam and Eve might have temporarily thought they had escaped the supposed consequence of their actions. They were still alive, after all. They had not been struck dead the moment they consumed the forbidden fruit. They thought they were alive, and they were right in a sense. They were physically alive, but inside, they were already spiritually dead. Their souls were empty of grace, the divine life of God. And physical death, the lesser of the two evils, would come for them in time.

After God found them and gave them their appropriate punishments, Adam and Eve were cast out of the Garden of Eden. They were sent out into the fallen world they had created through their sin, knowing they would never be allowed to return. They would no longer be able to walk with God in the cool of the evening. Their passage back into the Garden was blocked, and the way to the Tree of Life was barred. Why? The fall of man destroyed the relationship between man and God, separating man from the source of his divine life. If Adam and Eve had eaten of the Tree of Life in their fallen state, that separation would have become permanent. They would have lived forever, separated from God, in a hell of their own making. God didn't want that horrible existence for his beloved children, so he prevented them from becoming immortal until the time came for their salvation.[6]

Adam and Eve, and all mankind with them, have been doomed to the twofold death. We are all born spiritually dead, destined to physically die. We are dust, and to the dust we will return. We are born of the dust, lacking the breath of life that God breathed into Adam and Eve. We will all one day lose our lives to physical death, but we have also lost that divine spark that united us to God. If we are to be saved, life must be restored to both our bodies and our souls. Our death is twofold, so our healing must be twofold as well.

THE EFFECTS OF PHYSICAL AND SPIRITUAL DEATH

We are all born to die. Only a handful of people have been spared this consequence of original sin. In the Old Testament, both the

6   For more, see Mary Healy, *Men and Women Are from Eden: A Study Guide to John Paul II's Theology of the Body* (Cincinnati: Servant, 2005).

prophet Elijah and Enoch, the great-grandfather of Noah, were spared from the experience of physical death. Instead, they were carried away body and soul. The vast majority of us will face death at the end of our lives. Our souls will be separated from our bodies, and while our souls will stand before God for judgment, our bodies will be left on earth to decay, to return to the dust from which they were formed. For us, death is inevitable.[7]

But the physical consequences of death go beyond just the separation of body and soul. Physical death is often preceded by illness or injury. We age. Our cells may mutate and become cancerous. We physically suffer. Now that we have lost that original unity Adam and Eve possessed before the Fall, our bodies do not always cooperate. We are awkward, ungainly, unbalanced. We trip and tumble. We slip and slide. We try to jump, but our bodies come crashing down. We try to dance, but we trip over our own feet. We lack coordination, and the bumps and bruises are evidence of the disunity we all feel. But physical death is not even the worst of our punishment.

We are all born spiritually dead. Even as we breathe that first breath, we are dead inside. We lack the breath of life, the divine spirit given to Adam and Eve at their creation. While we continue to be made in the image of God, we now lack that divine likeness we once shared with our Creator. Not only is the unity between our bodies and souls broken, but the communion we once shared

---

7   See 2 Kings 2:11; Genesis 5:24; and Hebrews 11:5. In the New Testament, the most obvious example of someone whose body did not decay is Jesus Christ himself, who ascends body and soul to join his Father in heaven. The second example, which can only be inferred from Scripture, is Mary, who was assumed body and soul into heaven at the end of her life. Jesus Christ obviously died first, and he ascended to heaven only after rising from the dead. Even Mary is traditionally said to have "fallen asleep" before she was assumed, so as not to be deprived of any experience her son underwent. In these two unique cases, death was not a punishment for their sins, actual or original. Christ died to undo what Adam and Eve had done so that death would not be the end for us, and if Mary died, it was so that she could experience death just as her son did.

with God and with one another is gone too. And so we find ourselves at war—with God, with the world, with mankind, and with ourselves. When mankind fell from grace, death entered the world, bringing war, disease, and famine with it. Baptism restores our share in God's divine life, but it does not take away the other effects of original sin.

We are plagued by illness and injury but also concupiscence and temptation. We are broken inside, and that brokenness is reflected everywhere in the world. We are tempted to sin, to choose lesser goods when God offers us the best. Because of original sin, we often don't know what is best for us, and we don't believe God when he tries to tell us. We don't trust him, but we are the ones that we shouldn't trust. We are the broken ones, not God. We lie to ourselves and believe the lies of Satan, but God is Truth.

BROKEN IN MIND AND BODY

As a fallen race, we no longer enjoy that original unity experienced by Adam and Eve. Our relationships with God and with other people have suffered. Our communion with the opposite sex is broken. Our call to be stewards of this world has become a task of manipulation and mastering. Even within ourselves, we are fractured. Our very bodies and souls, essential to who we are as human persons, aren't united as they once were. Our bodies and souls, hearts and minds are often conflicted and confused.

And yet the link remains. Our bodies and souls are joined, united on a very fundamental level. We might be conflicted, but if the break was total, we would be dead. As long as we breathe, we are alive. Our bodies and souls are joined. Only death will fully separate the two, and until we breathe our last breath, our bodies and souls will share a conflicted connection. This is why we can be broken in our bodies and in our souls. We experience our brokenness in a unique way in the mind, where the body and soul merge. The mind is incredible. It is capable of so many amazing things, such as thinking, reasoning, choosing, and loving. These are the functions that make us uniquely human, that allow us to mirror the divine. In our fallen world, it should come as no surprise that the mind is also the source of many of our struggles.

For all of us, it can be difficult to recognize the truth at times. This is why we need to reform our minds by grace and the sacraments so that we can see clearly. For some of us, we need additional help to correct maladaptive thought processes. For those of us struggling with our mental health, the mind can be a very challenging place. I have looked in the mirror and convinced myself that I was fat, despite the fact that I was on the verge of being underweight. I have seen bulges and curves where there have only been straight lines and hollowed crevices. I have agonized over clothing choices in a desperate need to hide "flabby" arms, "muffin tops," and "stocky" thighs that didn't actually exist. (And so what if they had? Why shouldn't I still see myself as beautiful?) My mind has played all sorts of tricks on me. I have believed all sorts of lies about myself because my mind convinced me that they were the truth. Our ability to lie to ourselves, and to really believe those lies, is astounding.

The fall of man ushered in both physical and spiritual death. We can experience death in our bodies and our souls. Some of us are broken on the outside, but many more of us are broken on the inside. Countless women suffer from mental illness, ranging from body image issues to body dysmorphia, from depression and anxiety to eating disorders. We think our bodies are broken, but it's really our minds that are distorted or disordered. We hear the lies, and we believe them. We perpetuate the lies rather than admitting the truth. We are broken, but our brokenness is more than skin-deep.

When we are tempted to believe the lies about our bodies, we are tempted to disrespect and loathe the beautiful bodies God has given us. Satan likes nothing more than to amplify our brain's little lies until they are all that we are able to hear. Before long, we stop questioning the lies, and we believe that our bodies are just matter to be manipulated, that they are ugly lumps of flesh that can never be truly beautiful. It's so much easier for the Devil to wreak havoc in our souls when our minds are already working to convince us of the lies. He doesn't have much to do when our own minds are doing half the work for him. We don't want to distrust our minds, but if they are telling us lies, we need to seek the Truth and find the spiritual and psychological healing that we need.

HEALING OUR BROKENNESS

Healing the wounds in our minds will often take more than just prayer. We won't be able to just pray our struggles away. I spent years assuming that I wasn't praying hard enough. I thought that if I just prayed more, I would be healed. I assumed that if I remained ill, it was because I wasn't trying hard enough. I wasn't holy enough. I wasn't good enough. Ironically, the more seriously I took my faith, the worse my eating disorder and body image issues became. I convinced myself that I was still struggling because I simply wasn't good enough. Once again, I was not enough.

After nearly a decade of struggling, I realized the truth. My struggle wasn't just a spiritual problem. It was a physical problem. My body issues were as much about my body as they were about my soul. If I wanted to find healing, I needed to treat both my body and my soul. Spiritually, prayer never hurts, and speaking with a spiritual director can work wonders. But often, prayer is just not enough.

In addition to prayer and emotional support from family and friends, those of us who suffer with eating disorders and body image issues will often need to turn to psychologists, psychiatrists, nutritionists, and wellness experts for help. We will need to seek healing for our souls as well as our brains. For some of us, emotional support and some research on health, nutrition, and exercise will get us on the path to healing. For others, professional help will be needed. There is nothing wrong with saying that prayer and spiritual direction are not enough. God gave us doctors for a reason. He created us to be embodied, and so he also gave us the means to heal those bodies. And our brains are as much a part of our bodies as our hands or feet are.

Personally, I never saw a therapist, though I suspect if I had, I would have begun my journey to healing much earlier than I actually did. I definitely would have benefited from seeing a therapist, if only because I would have been able to share my struggles with someone else. I kept my eating disorder a secret for so long, and I refused to consider counseling because that would have meant admitting that I had a problem. Unfortunately for me, pride kept me from seeking help for nearly a decade. I only considered methods of healing that allowed me to hide my eating disorder, but without any accountability, none of my attempts at healing survived my Saturday night binge. I was never meant to suffer alone, and I was never meant to heal alone, either. I needed a community for support and accountability, but I refused to accept that fact for a very long time. I believed that if I prayed hard enough and worked hard enough, I would be able to heal myself. Pride came before the fall of Adam and Eve, but it was present in my fall as well.

God created us with bodies and souls, and he gave us the means to find both physical and spiritual healing. But if we want to find healing for our bodies and minds, we need to learn how our bodies and minds are meant to work. If we understand how our bodies are supposed to function, we can better see where they are broken. And once we've identified the problem, we can start working toward a solution. If our problem is in our brains, where our bodies and souls mingle in a very unique way, then we will most likely need to seek both physical and spiritual methods of healing. We must pray and learn about fitness and nutrition; we must seek out spiritual directors and therapists.

My journey to healing began after a decade of struggling and fear. I was afraid to admit I had a problem, afraid to admit I wasn't perfect. I was too proud to destroy the carefully crafted facade of perfection I had created. If I admitted that I was struggling with an eating disorder, I would need to admit that I was broken. I would need to admit that the perfect porcelain doll was actually broken, even if you couldn't see the cracks. But then, hiding in my bedroom and binging at ten p.m., I hit rock bottom and realized that if I was ever going to escape the hole I had created for myself, I would need help. So after hiding my brokenness for more than ten years, I finally admitted that I couldn't heal myself. And do you know what? No one abandoned me. No one wrote me off because I was broken. In the end, I had never been a porcelain doll; I had always been human, and all humans are capable of falling. But the good news? We might be fallen, but we have also been redeemed.

QUESTIONS FOR REFLECTION

1. Have you ever felt close to God and yet far away from him at the same time? Why did you feel that way?

2. What was at the core of the original sin of Adam and Eve?

3. What were the consequences of the original sin? What is the twofold curse of death?

4. What lies has Satan whispered into your mind? How have you responded to those whispers?

5. Where are your favorite places to go to seek spiritual and physical healing?

An Exercise in Seeing Yourself as God Does

NOTICING YOUR THOUGHTS AND GIVING THEM TO GOD

In this chapter, we discussed how our unhelpful thoughts can act as barriers that prevent us from living peacefully and focusing on God's plan for our lives. Because our mind is designed to think, it is almost constantly producing thoughts. It can be helpful to create distance from our thoughts so we can see them for what they are and choose our next actions intentionally, rather than be pushed and pulled by thoughts all day long.

One helpful strategy for gaining space from your thoughts is to label them *as* thoughts. For example, when your mind begins offering you critical thoughts about your body, such as, "My body is too big," or, "I hate how I look," simply restate these thoughts with the added stem: "I am having the thought that ..." So, for example, you might say, "I am having the thought that my body is too big," or, "I am having the thought that I hate how I look." Over time, it will become easier to see these thoughts for what they are—thoughts!—rather than factual statements about yourself.

5

Our Broken Bodies

In the depths of my struggles with an eating disorder, I liked to pretend that I was a soldier going off to war. It helped me to justify my behavior to myself, even though my routines were just further evidence of the depths of the lies and my disordered thinking. If I was fighting to be victorious in battle, all of my suffering seemed to have meaning. Every morning, I would wake up and prepare myself mentally to face the enemy. I would think through the day's events, considering my future battles and chances of success. My enemy was powerful and possessed many faces. Food was the enemy. The mirror was the enemy. Other women were the enemy. The scale was the enemy. My body was the enemy. I needed to conquer the many evils in my life, and the war needed to be fought from the moment I woke up each morning to the moment I fell asleep at night. The war was never-ending, but I was a good soldier, and I kept fighting.

Every morning, I donned my "armor." As I pulled on my running gear, I planned my workouts for the day. I had a daily regimen of exercise that I adhered to religiously because I was afraid that if I let myself slack, I would lose the war against my body. I told myself that I needed to be fit and in control if I was going to fight well. My workouts were my way of ensuring that I would be victorious in the war my mind had created.

I had plenty of little "victories"—a pound lost, a dropped dress size, a compliment on the street. I felt like I was winning plenty of battles, but every night, by the time I went to bed, I still felt like I was losing the war. Because at the end of the day, even if that day had been filled with "victories," I still hated myself. I was still a loser. My mind told me that I still wasn't good enough, pretty enough, skinny enough. The lies of my disorder were loud and accusatory, and it was nearly impossible to hear anything else. The din of battle had deafened me to the whispers of God attempting to speak the truth into my heart.

I fought the war against myself for nearly ten years. That's a lot of fighting, especially when your primary enemy is yourself. Sure, I blamed food for my struggles, but I was the one who couldn't control myself. I blamed modern society, with its Barbie dolls and skinny models, but I was the one who wanted to be as "beautiful" and "feminine" as Barbie. Yes, I felt like I was at war with food, and the world, and God, but more than anything, I was at war with myself. So I fought to be stronger. I fought for control. I beat myself down until I was too weak to fight. And every morning, I donned my armor, like the good little solder I was.

SINNERS IN HIDING

Then the eyes of both were opened, and they knew that they were naked; and they sewed fig leaves together and made themselves aprons.

And they heard the sound of the LORD God walking in the garden in the cool of the day, and the man and his wife hid themselves from the presence of the LORD God among the trees of

the garden. But the LORD God called to the man,
and said to him, "Where are you?" And he said, "I
heard the sound of you in the garden, and I was
afraid, because I was naked; and I hid myself."
He said, "Who told you that you were naked?"
(Genesis 3:7–11)

If there is one Scripture passage that inevitably rattles me to my core when I read it, this is it. I was naked, so I hid myself. I used to spend a lot of time in hiding. I hid my body in loose-fitting clothes. I hid my binging in the confines of my bedroom. I hid my exercise habits in the early hours of the morning and the wee hours of night. I hid my illness behind my perfectly constructed facade. I tried to hide myself from God and from every person who might have offered me help. I saw that I was broken, so I hid myself. I was ashamed, so I hid myself.

The moment that Adam and Eve consume the fruit, their eyes are opened and they see that they are naked. They lose that original innocence they had before the Fall. When they look at each other, they don't just see a person to be loved at all times. Now their eyes are tinted with lust, and they also see an object to be used for their own gratification. They don't want to just love each other; they want to use each other. And so they hide.

Adam and Eve want to hide from themselves and from each other just as much as they want to hide from God. They are ashamed. And like any child who is ashamed after disobeying his or her father, Adam and Eve hide. As if they can really hide from God. Then, to make matters worse, when God gives Adam and Eve the opportunity to fess up to their disobedience, they choose to blame others for their actions. Adam blames Eve; Eve blames the Serpent. In reality, all three of them are at fault, and they all must face the consequences for their actions.

Because of the Fall, we have lost the communion we once shared with all of creation and with God himself. We are broken inside, and our brokenness can be seen in our relationships with other people, particularly those of the opposite sex. We have ceased to be caretakers of this world that we have been given, opting instead to manipulate it in our attempts to control it. And worst of all, we have separated ourselves from God. Born in sin, we lack that divine life that once connected us to God. Even after receiving the grace of Baptism, where that divine life is restored to us, we continue to make choices that weaken or even destroy our relationship with God. We have been redeemed, but we are still plagued by the consequences of that original sin.

BROKEN IN BODY AND SOUL

The relationship between our body and soul has become fractured as a result of the Fall. It is not a complete break—we are not dead yet, after all, but it *is* a profound injury. We experience discord where there was once communion, disharmony where there was once perfect balance. "The spirit indeed is willing, but the flesh is weak," as Jesus says (Matthew 26:41). We want to do good, but we don't. We want to avoid evil, but we sin anyway. We are weak. We are conflicted. The spirit is willing, but the flesh is weak.

We have also stopped viewing ourselves as embodied souls. In our own eyes, now we are just souls with temporary bodies. Or we are just temporary bodies, doomed to nonexistence after death. We think our bodies are something we possess. We no longer are our bodies; we have them. We use them. We control them.

We manipulate them to be what we want them to be. We try to force them into the molds we have in our heads, as if our bodies were Play-Doh that we could shape as we see fit.

When we reduce the human body to just matter to be manipulated, we forget what our bodies are supposed to mean to us. They stop mattering to us. Our bodies lose their value. And if we think they have no value, we stop treating them with respect. Our flesh becomes something we use and discard when we're done. We can cut it, fill it, mold it, or let it waste away until it's something entirely new. We think our bodies don't make us "us," so they don't matter. But we're wrong.

Our bodies do matter. They are ours to cherish, to nourish, to protect. They are a gift from God, a blessing that we bear so that we can experience all there is to this life. And like any gift that we are given, the appropriate response is gratitude. But what does it mean to be grateful for our bodies? How are we supposed to show God that we are thankful for what he has given us? Gratitude means that we must receive our gift as something that belongs to us but is also an extension of the one who gave it to us. Because whenever we are given a gift, we are given a bit of the giver. Children understand and live this out in a very clear way. When my son gives me a hand-painted picture, it becomes mine. But if I take that picture and throw it in the trash, how do you think my son would respond? Not well, obviously. The picture might belong to me now, but my son put something of himself into that painting when he created it. If I were to reject the picture, in a very real way I would be rejecting him. My son made himself vulnerable when he gave me that painting; he knew I could reject it. He knew I could reject him. But he gave me the picture anyway. Why? Because he loves me.

God feels the same way about our bodies. When we were given our bodies, we were given something of God. Our bodies were meant to reveal something of who God is to the world. Our bodies are not just meaningless matter but possess the divine spark of God's love within them. When God created us, he breathed his own divine life into us. We are temples of the Holy Spirit, tabernacles that house the living presence of God. In loving our bodies, we love God. And when we spit on our bodies, when we treat them like meaningless matter, we spit on the face of God.

Our broken view of our bodies is the result of the brokenness of our souls. We are broken inside, so we see brokenness on the outside. We see flaws. We see imperfections. We see scars, stretch marks, and unacceptable curves. We see wrinkles, bags under our eyes, and puffy cheeks. We see ourselves as ugly. But we can't see past our sin-tinted glasses; we don't see ourselves the way God does.

God sees the marks of a life being lived, and hopefully lived well. He sees proof that we have chosen to give ourselves to our loved ones. If we are biological mothers, he sees evidence of our physical motherhood, of the life-giving miracle he worked inside us. He sees all the moments of joy that led to laugh lines and wrinkles around our eyes. He sees the late nights and early mornings we sacrificed for the people and passions that mean the most to us. God sees beauty when he looks at us, and he possesses a clarity that we cannot fathom. He sees all truth, and the truth is that we are beautiful and loved. Unfortunately, in our brokenness, we struggle to believe him. We are ashamed of our brokenness, so we hide. We hide from God, and we hide from ourselves.

THE TEMPTATION TO USE AND ABUSE

We also hide from each other. After Adam and Eve eat the fruit, they hide. They hide from God, true, but they also want to hide from each other. They want to cover themselves. After God gives them their respective punishments, he grants them one last mercy before banishing them from Eden—he gives them garments to cover themselves. The clothing isn't for hiding themselves from God (though they may think it can serve that purpose, too), but it allows them to conceal something of themselves from each other. Shame leads them to cover themselves.

The fall of man ushers in the age-old temptation to objectification. Adam looks at Eve and sees an object to be used for his own gratification. He still loves her, but he lusts after her too. When Adam looks at Eve, he sees his wife, but he also sees a means to receive bodily pleasure. Their relationship is not as pure as it once was.

Many of us know what it feels like to be used, as well as how it feels to use. In school, we were tempted to befriend straight A students in the hopes that their friendship would also help our own grades. We were friendly with them, but we also used them to our own advantage. As we get older, we become more skilled at using people to get what we want. We might be tempted to use members of the opposite sex to satisfy our own desires for love or just sex. Even our purest friendships can be tainted by the desire to use people to get what we want. As a stay-at-home mom, I want distractions that will make my days pass more quickly and with more enjoyment. So I befriend other moms with children the same age as my own. Our friendship is genuine, but it has also stemmed from a personal need or desire. We don't want to be lonely. We don't want to be bored. So we look for people to keep us company, to entertain us. Luckily, true friendships—the kind where we put the other person's well-being first—can still arise from these utilitarian beginnings. Our needs and desires are conflicted, but they can be purified.

As women, many of us know how it feels to be used by the opposite sex. Countless women have recounted loveless relationships where their boyfriends were "just in it for the sex." They have felt like objects, a means to carnal pleasure. I remember being in college and debating the pros and cons of premarital sex and cohabitation. A classmate argued that these were both helpful because "you would never buy a car without test-driving it first." I was shocked to hear myself or any woman compared to a car, and even more shocked to see the sheer number of men who felt that this objectification of women was both good and necessary. Many women are familiar with the feeling of being undressed mentally when a man leers at her. We are left feeling dirty and disposable. We feel replaceable and interchangeable. We feel used.

But we're not all innocent either. Some of us will use men the same way, to appease our sexual desires. Others will use men so that they can feel loved. In my years as a youth minister, I had more than one teenager admit that they didn't care who they were with, as long as they were with *someone*. They didn't want a relationship with a particular man; they just wanted a relationship. Some of us might even be tempted to "test-drive the car," as my classmate suggested. The boys in my class were not the only ones who felt that it was OK to test out sex and living together before the arrangement became too permanent. But mutual objectification is still objectification.

Women can be tempted to use men, but more often than not, I think the greater temptation is for women to use other women. Whenever we compare ourselves and knock other women down in our minds (or with our words), we are using other women. We are using them to make ourselves feel better. When we compare ourselves to other women, when we catalog their features and compare them to our own, we are using each other. When we knock others down to build ourselves up, we are using each other. And every time we use each other, this is just further proof that our relationships are broken and that our unity with the rest of humanity has been lost.

The breaking of unity that came with the Fall brought shame with it. No one likes to be used. No one wants to be treated like an object. No one wants to feel exposed and vulnerable in this broken world. So we hide ourselves. We cover up. We look to protect ourselves. Shame is an effect of sin, but it also protects us from the consequences of the Fall. It serves as a reminder that we are not meant to be used. We are made for more than that.

LIVING IN A BROKEN WORLD

We find ourselves at war with the world as often as we are at war with ourselves. Our disordered thinking tells us to blame ourselves for our lack of control, for our weakness, for our disobedient bodies, but we also blame the world. We blame the photoshopped models, the disfigured Barbie dolls, and the simple temptation of food. We tell ourselves that these are the enemies. We convince ourselves that though our bodies are weak, it's the world that really takes advantage of our weakness.

And it's true. Our society loves its photoshopped images and unrealistic proportions. It loves perfection and impossible flawlessness. And it loves reminding us that we are not perfect, that we are not flawless. And so we are left blaming ourselves. We are left blaming our uncooperative bodies. For some of us, we are left blaming our need for food, our body's need for nourishment. In the end, food becomes just another enemy.

But food was never meant to be our enemy. Food gives us life. It provides nourishment to our bodies and fuel to get through each day of life. Without food, we would die. God gave us food so that we could live. He created food because he knew we would need it. And as something made by God, food is good. It's a gift, given to us by God so that we might live. Man might not live by bread alone, but he would certainly die without it.

As an essential source of sustenance, food is good. Part of my recovery process included accepting this truth about food. I used to separate food into "good" and "bad." Salad, vegetables, lean meats—those were all very good foods. Candies, chocolate, and baked goods were all bad. I ate it all, but the bad foods were all evil temptations that wouldn't leave me alone. It took me a very long time to change my thinking and learn the virtue of temperance, which "provides balance in the use of created goods" (CCC 1809). Even now, I occasionally catch myself reverting to good/bad categories. Just a few months ago, I was teaching my son about the food pyramid. He was supposed to separate foods into their appropriate categories, and when it came time to put the cookies and candies at the top, I caught myself calling them "bad." I quickly backtracked and corrected myself, reminding both of us that we are meant to enjoy sweets in moderation. But we really are supposed to *enjoy* them. And if a food is meant to be enjoyed, it must be good.

But food is more than just fuel for our flesh or something to be enjoyed by our senses. Our flesh is more than just matter; our bodies are essential to who we are as human persons. That means that eating is more than just the consumption and breaking down of nutrients for the proper functioning of the body. There is a reason that we gather for meals, that we indulge in delicious desserts, that the best parties and activities include food. Even our worship involves eating. God actually becomes physical food for us. He tells us to eat his Body. Eating is an experience for us, not just a task. It is communion. It is life-giving. And in the Eucharist, God gives life both to our bodies and to our souls. He feeds us physically and spiritually. God becomes our food.

Jesus Christ has shown the goodness of our bodies and food. He has chosen to exist in both forms. Two thousand years ago, he became incarnate in a human body. He spent thirty-three years in that body before he died and rose again. He liked his body so much that he took it with him when he returned to heaven. He liked it so much that he didn't want to go home without it. He brought it with him—because it *was* him, just as much as his human soul and his divine spirit were him.

But God didn't stop there. Jesus didn't just become human for us. He became food for us. Jesus invites us to eat his Body and drink his Blood. God desires to unite himself with us, so he did it by becoming what we eat. He became food so that his very Body and Blood could join with ours. He became food so that his divinity could mingle with our humanity. He became food so that we might become what we eat. Food can't possibly be the true enemy if God is willing to become the very thing that so many of us dread. By becoming food, God gives us definitive proof that food is not bad. It's actually good, and it's so good that in the Eucharist, food becomes divine.

BECOMING A SOLDIER FOR CHRIST

I spent years assuming that food was the enemy, that my body was the enemy, that the culture was the enemy. I was mostly wrong. Food was a source of temptation for me, but it was not evil. My body was weak, but it was not bad. And the culture might prey on my weakness and concupiscence, but it merely hid the true enemy behind its glittery, airbrushed facade. I am at war, but it is not food, my body, or the world that I am fighting against. It is temptation. It is sin. It is Satan. I have always been a soldier, but I spent a decade fighting the wrong enemy. You might even say that I was fighting for the Enemy.

Now I know that I am a soldier for Christ. I am a warrior of God, and I must don my armor every day in my war against Satan. As St. Paul writes,

> *Finally, be strong in the Lord and in the strength of his might. Put on the whole armor of God, that you may be able to stand against the wiles of the devil. For we are not contending against flesh and blood, but against the principalities, against the powers, against the world rulers of this present darkness, against the spiritual hosts of wickedness in the heavenly places. Therefore take the whole armor of God, that you may be able to withstand in the evil day, and having done all, to stand. Stand therefore, having fastened the belt of truth around your waist, and having put on the breastplate of righteousness, and having shod your feet with the equipment of the gospel of peace; besides all these, taking the shield of faith, with which you can quench all the flaming darts of the Evil One. And take the helmet of salvation, and the sword of the Spirit, which is the word of God. (Ephesians 6:10–17)*

We are all called to fight. We are called to grow in the virtue of temperance, to practice self-discipline, and to prepare ourselves spiritually for the battle ahead. As the *Catechism* tells us, "*temperance* is the moral virtue that moderates the attraction of pleasures and provides balance in the use of created goods ... The temperate person directs the sensitive appetites toward what is good and maintains a healthy discretion" (CCC 1809). The *Catechism* goes on to quote the book of Sirach: "Do not follow your [own] inclination and strength" (Sirach 5:2). I still enjoy running, but I know my running attire is not my true armor. Now I turn for strength to God in prayer. Now I wear the Scriptures, wash my weapons in the blood and water of the sacraments, and shield myself with the prayers of the Catholic Faith. But I can also eat cake, a cookie, or a second roll at dinner when I choose. Because food is not the enemy, and I was created by a God who ate and drank with his friends, who celebrated weddings with wine, and who thought food was so important that when he wanted to become one with us, he did it by becoming food for us. Jesus Christ became man so that we might become like God, and he became food so that we might become what we eat.

QUESTIONS FOR REFLECTION

1. Why are we sometimes led to desire things that are not good for us? Why do we sometimes fail to seek after those things that will draw us closer to God?

2. Have you ever used another person for your own pleasure or other personal need? What are the dangers inherent in using another person as an object for personal gratification?

3. How might you work to purify a utilitarian friendship?

4. What is the significance of Christ's decision to become food for us? How does it change the way that we are meant to look at food?

5. Who is the real enemy in this spiritual war that we are all fighting? What is the armor that we are called to don in the battle for our souls?

An Exercise in Seeing Yourself as God Does

CULTIVATING "WILLINGNESS"

We are often tempted to hide from difficulty or use others as a way of avoiding internal experiences that are uncomfortable or hard to tolerate. For example, when Adam and Eve hid from God in the Garden, they likely wanted to avoid the discomfort of admitting their wrongdoing. When we use others, it is often an attempt to change uncomfortable feelings we are having, such as loneliness or sadness. If we are able to better tolerate the discomfort we experience without rushing to change our feelings, we can make choices that are better aligned with our identities as adopted children of God. One strategy for increasing our ability to tolerate discomfort is by intentionally opening ourselves up to experience our thoughts, feelings, and sensations as they are in the moment without trying to change or control them; this is called "willingness." Consider using this strategy to help understand how "willingness" can be helpful.

1. Get a pen and a piece of paper. Call to mind a recent experience where you wish you had acted differently, and write it down.

2. Reflect on this experience: What were you feeling at the time? Do you remember what thoughts you were having? Were you feeling uncomfortable? Anxious? Afraid? Ashamed? Make a note of the thoughts and feelings you recall from your experience.

3. Consider how these internal experiences dictated the actions you chose to take. Were you trying to escape an uncomfortable feeling? Were you trying to quiet a troubling thought?

4. Think about how you might have behaved if you had been willing to experience that internal discomfort. What would you have done or said? Imagine in detail what it would look like to have chosen "willingness" in this situation.

6

Motherhood in a Fallen World

I have never felt more beautiful than when I was pregnant with my two children. I *loved* being pregnant. Sure, the nausea wasn't great, and I didn't enjoy the labor part very much, but I really loved pregnancy. I felt feminine. I felt womanly. I felt beautiful. I loved the feeling of my children growing inside me. I felt surprisingly comfortable in my body, a feeling that was completely foreign to me. It probably had something to do with the fact that I was actually supposed to gain weight, that it was expected and even applauded. It was a very new concept for me.

I know many women have a very different experience of pregnancy. They face swollen ankles and puffy faces, swollen fingers and ever-expanding, uncomfortable bellies. Sitting and standing become an incredible struggle, and they adopt the "penguin waddle" way of walking that is so common among pregnant women. They feel fat, ugly, and unfamiliar with their own bodies. They are sore and exhausted, and that's all before the actual labor and delivery part begins.

My labors did not have complications. They both lasted about twelve hours from first contraction to time of birth. Both of my children were born in the same hospital, but with different doctors, and both labors were unmedicated (though I was *very* close to getting an epidural with my second). By six weeks postpartum, I was pretty well healed, though I still felt uncomfortable in my postpartum body. By now, I've come to realize that my body most likely won't be the same again. It's been through too much to remain unchanged by what has happened.

I know many women who have endured insanely long, incredibly painful labors. I know women who have undergone severe trauma during delivery, and many who have needed a C-section after hours of laboring. I know women who nearly died in the process of giving birth, or who have lost their children after months of carrying them in their wombs and hours of laboring to bring them into this world. I know women who have needed months to physically heal from the experience, and some who have needed years to mentally recover. But no matter how we bring our children into the world, we are changed forever.

WOMAN'S PUNISHMENT FOR HER ORIGINAL SIN

> *To the woman he said, "I will greatly multiply your pain in childbearing; in pain you shall bring forth children, yet your desire shall be for your husband, and he shall rule over you." (Genesis 3:16)*

After the first sin of Adam and Eve, God bestows on man and woman punishments appropriate to who they are as human persons. For Eve, these punishments speak to who she is as a woman and as a mother. Her innate desire to give herself to her husband will be skewed by sin. She will seek not only to love him but to control him. Her relationship with her husband will be tainted by warring wills and a need for control. Men will dominate, and women, in their desire for love and sometimes power, will allow themselves to be controlled. And of course now childbirth, one of the most incredible experiences in a woman's life, will be tainted by pain and suffering.

Childbirth was always part of God's plan for mankind. He had always intended that women have the miraculous gift of pregnancy and childbirth, the ability to bring life into the world after having carried that life within them. Motherhood is at the core of woman's femininity, so it was only appropriate that Eve's punishment be related to her call to be a mother. And because motherhood is so innate, the pain of childbirth has not deterred women from answering the God-given call to become physical mothers through pregnancy and childbirth.

ENDURING THE PHYSICAL PAIN OF CHILDBIRTH

Many women describe childbirth as the most painful experience they've ever had. It certainly was for me, and I've broken bones so badly that I needed multiple surgeries to repair them. I've taken multiple softballs to the face. I endured years of debilitating migraines as a teenager. But none of those experiences can compare to the pain of childbirth. And yet for some reason, the pain I suffered the first time didn't stop me from doing it again. The gift of children is worth all the pain I've endured in childbirth. It seems crazy, but I also know plenty of women who feel the same way. If you're a mother yourself, you might, as well.

Even though pain in childbirth was a punishment for the sinfulness of humanity, God has not left us alone in our suffering. When Adam and Eve saw that they were naked and sought to cover themselves, God replaced their fig leaves with animal hide. Similarly, God did not abandon men in their vocation to protect and provide, and he did not leave women to suffer the pains of childbirth unsupported. Women possess the unfathomable ability to endure the pain of childbirth. We endure it, and we invite it back. We welcome it for the sake of our children.

Women were created strong enough to face the suffering that accompanies labor and the delivery of our children. We were gifted with a high tolerance for pain, an endurance that is incomparable, and a willingness to suffer for the sake of those we love. We are even willing to suffer for those souls who do not yet exist, souls that we hope will become embodied within us, souls that will be given life and limb in our wombs. They might only exist in our minds and hearts, but we are already ready and willing to suffer for them. We will accept the pain in exchange for their lives, for their chance to live.

ENDURING THE EMOTIONAL AND PSYCHOLOGICAL PAIN OF CHILDBIRTH

Pregnancy and childbirth is generally physically exhausting, but it can also be emotionally draining. Many women struggle with postpartum depression and/or anxiety (PPD/PPA), and these conditions can also be found in pregnant women on occasion as well. Body image issues can become more intense during pregnancy and the months following childbirth. Just as women who suffered from anxiety or depression before pregnancy are more likely to be diagnosed with PPD/PPA, women who have suffered with body image issues prior to having children are more likely to experience exacerbated symptoms during and after pregnancy.

Despite my history of body image issues and an eating disorder, I absolutely loved being pregnant. I loved how I felt. I loved the freedom that came with not having to worry about my weight, or about food, or about whether a too-large dinner would make me look fat in my dress. For the sake of my unborn child, I was eating healthily and exercising regularly. I was establishing new habits, and by the time my first child was born, I was happy with how I felt and how I looked, even though my body felt softer and more rounded than it had before. In the weeks and months following the birth of my son, the change in weight did not matter as much as the amount of energy I had as well as the overall sense of contentment. I had experienced that my body was created with a purpose, and even if it wasn't fitting the world's standard of "beauty," I knew my body was beautiful. I felt good, and I wanted to preserve that feeling.

As it turned out, my new habits probably had a lot to do with my eventual conquering of postpartum depression and anxiety. During my first few months as a mother, I was plagued by feelings of inadequacy, regret, and anxiety. I was haunted by phantom cries at night, which were accompanied by the very real cries of my son, who refused to sleep. I often woke up feeling as if I couldn't breathe, as if my very life was being choked out of me because of the smothering presence of my son. We were both sleep-deprived, exhausted, and desperate for comfort. My newfound healthy eating and exercise habits, as well as prayer and communication with my husband, were my shining beacons of hope in the midst of the darkness of postpartum anxiety.

Much of my anxiety centered on my son's sleeping and eating habits. He wasn't a great sleeper, even as newborns go, and I was just not prepared for the devastating effects of sleep deprivation. I was up with him multiple times throughout the night, and the task of getting him back to sleep after a nighttime feed seemed nearly impossible. Even after my son was sleeping again, sometimes I would remain awake for hours, listening to the phantom cries

I heard coming from the other room. I could not close my eyes against the glow of the monitor because I just *knew* that the moment I fell asleep, the phantom cries would become real and my son would need me again.

The days were not much better than the nights. I had opted to breastfeed my son, a choice I made because of a combination of peer pressure, coercion from the "breast is best" campaign, and a deep-seated need to be just like everyone else. It took me less than a day to realize that I absolutely hated nursing, but it still took me about a month before I finally found the strength and self-confidence needed to make the switch to formula. I hated breastfeeding, but I considered quitting a sign of my failure. If I quit, it was proof that I wasn't a good enough mother to my son. The ugly whispers that told me that I wasn't good enough came back with a vengeance, and I felt helpless against them. So for an entire month, I refused to quit, even though I was miserable. I lived in fear of the clock, counting down the hours and minutes until the next feed, or the next nap. I occasionally suffered from panic attacks as those final minutes before the next feed or nap ticked by. I would be reading or working on my computer when I would notice the time, and suddenly my throat would tighten up and I would find myself desperately trying to suck air into my heaving lungs. I was suffering immensely, but I was also stubborn. I did not want to be a failure.

As the days passed, I slowly gave in to my desire for peace. I still thought that giving up was a sign of my failure as a mother, but I just couldn't handle it anymore. I was drowning, and I needed to get to shore before it was too late. After a month of nursing, I told my husband I was only going to nurse at night. A week later, my son was entirely bottle-fed. When my son was four months old, divine providence intervened, rescuing me from my sleep struggles—I threw out my back. It was probably the best thing that could have happened to me. Since I was unable to rock my son to sleep, my husband and I turned to gentle sleep training. A week later, he was sleeping relatively well in his crib, and I could finally see the sun peeking out behind the dark clouds of those newborn days. But it still took an entire year for the phantom cries to finally cease and for peace to finally reign in my life again.

By the time my daughter was born two and a half years later, I knew what triggered my anxiety, and I knew how to best avoid or address those triggers. I also had a much deeper appreciation for how amazing my body was. While I had spent my first pregnancy learning about proper nutrition and healthy exercise, I was able to really appreciate the power of my body the second time around. My body was sustaining the life of my child. She was growing inside me, drawing my flesh and blood into her little body. We were one, but also two. We were united, but also distinct. God had blessed me with the incredible gift of pregnancy, the ability to have new life take form and grow within me. And when the time came, God gave me the grace, strength, and perseverance to give birth to my daughter.

When I left the hospital, my body felt a bit lighter, but my arms were seven lbs., two oz. heavier. When I returned home, my stomach was still swollen and empty, but my arms were full. And my heart was full. For the first few weeks home, that was all that mattered. Our bodies are capable of near miracles and incredible feats. They can hold life where there once was none, and they can endure hours and even days of pain and suffering to bring that life into the world. I was in awe of my body, amazed by its abilities, its strength, its power. I was just too amazed by my body to fault it for anything.

EMBRACING YOUR NEW MOTHER'S BODY

Of course, there eventually came a point when the temptation to berate myself returned. As the months passed, it became harder to ignore the changes to my body. Even after months of eating well and exercising, my body still didn't look the same. As my daughter's first birthday approached, I realized a very important truth—some post-pregnancy changes to the body are long-lasting. It didn't matter that I had returned to my pre-pregnancy weight. It didn't matter that I ate well and exercised regularly. My hips remained wider, and the small bump on my abdomen never fully receded, no matter how much I exercised. My body never returned to its pre-pregnancy state, and I was occasionally tempted to berate myself for the apparent flaws I saw in it.

In the depths of my heart, I have come to accept that some of the changes that come with pregnancy are permanent. After having undergone such an incredible, life-changing experience, how could I not be changed? I was certainly changed on the inside, so why shouldn't I also be changed on the outside? Our hearts expand and change with the births of our children, so it shouldn't come as a surprise that our bodies change too.

Our bodies are the reflection of our souls. Our souls are affected by the births of our children. Our hearts grow, and our capacity for love expands. With each child, our hearts make room to love another child. With each child, our hearts are overwhelmed by new life and love. Our hearts stretch thin, but they do not break. They only become capable of more love. Each pregnancy does the same for our bodies.

With each pregnancy, each child, our bodies change. Our wombs make room for another child to live and grow. Our skin stretches taut, but it does not break. Our bodies are meant to carry life within them, and our skin is designed to stretch and engulf, to provide shelter to the child living inside us. Our hips expand to allow our children access to this world, but our widened hips also allow us to carry those children in our arms and against our bodies. Our curves provide our children physical and emotional comfort, a place where they can bury their heads when they are scared or upset.

Our bodies are designed so that we can love our children with our entire being, but sin often leads us to see our bodies as scarred and deformed rather than beautiful and powerful. We might step onto the scale happy with how we look and feel, and then completely change our minds after we see the number. Now we feel fat. We see the stretch marks on our skin, and it doesn't matter that up until that moment we felt comfortable. Now we feel ugly. We are tempted to focus on how we look and to find fault with it. But we don't see ourselves the way God sees us. Our vision is clouded by sin, and we lose sight of how incredible our bodies truly are.

WOMAN'S "URGE" FOR HER HUSBAND

In addition to the pain of childbirth, women were cursed with a broken relationship with men, particularly within marriage. Women will seek to control and manipulate men, and men will do the same, albeit with arguably more success. Women will seek to dominate their husbands, leading to a war of wills that has little room for love. And woman, in her need for love, will often find herself dominated. She will seek control, but her husband will rule over her. She will lose.

We see this disrupted relationship between men and women all the time. Power struggles exist in all walks of life, and women have sought to demean other women and emasculate men in their need to dominate. Women permit men to use them as objects in the hopes of gaining power. They sell themselves, offer favors, agree to be objectified, all in the hopes of rising. And no one cares who has to fall in the process. They falsely believe that the only way to gain power is by taking it from others.

We see the disruption played out in marriage and family life as well. Men and women were created as equals, but there is always a temptation to act as superiors and inferiors. Husbands and wives fight for control, causing the entire family to suffer. They are both tempted to use each other, to use their children, and to use their very bodies and the gift of sex as leverage. They are willing to sacrifice themselves and each other for the sake of power and domination. But their sacrifices never amount to anything, and the entire family will continue to suffer.

God calls us to rise above the temptation, but we will never rise by tearing one another down. We can only rise together, by lifting each other up and offering assistance to those who might fall. We were made for communion after all, and in marriage, we are called to support our husbands. We are called to sacrifice for the sake of the other, trusting that our husbands will sacrifice themselves for us as well. If we all give, then we will all receive, and we will never be left empty. Our souls will always be filled to the point of overflowing.

FINDING BEAUTY IN THE MIDST OF SUFFERING

I didn't feel particularly beautiful as I labored to give birth to either of my children. After twelve hours of increasingly painful contractions, I felt sweaty, tired, and miserable. I was ready to meet my child, to see the reason for all my pain and suffering face-to-face. I knew that once I could hold my baby in my arms, all of the pain would be worthwhile. And as any mother might guess, I was right.

When you're in the midst of labor, the idea of having another child seems ridiculous. You might tell your husband that you're done having kids, that one is enough, that you would never put yourself through this pain again. You might even blame your husband for your current situation (you couldn't have done it without him, after all). Then you meet your child, and the pain is suddenly worth it—but you still tell yourself that you will never do it again. A few months later, the memories have softened, and you can't look at a baby without feeling the pull for "just one more." And like countless women around the world, you find yourself pregnant again, despite everything you originally said.

The pull to be a mother is strong. Baby fever is real, rooted in memories and the sweet smell of newborns. Despite the pain, despite the hours of labor and the weeks of recovery, we find ourselves willing to do it again. As our memories get fuzzy and our children grow into themselves, the pain doesn't seem so bad. It's certainly not enough to stop many of us from doing it again. As my husband and I discerned whether it was time to welcome another child into our family, the pain of childbirth never fit into the equation. My struggle with postpartum anxiety did. The sleepless nights did. Our living arrangements did. But I was more than willing to endure the pain of labor for the sake of another child.

The pain of childbirth might be a curse as a result of the original sin of mankind, but that doesn't stop women from rising to the occasion time and time again. God gives us the perseverance to push through the pain. He gives us the strength to face that pain more than once. And he gives us our mothers' hearts, hearts that are willing to endure all sorts of pain and suffering for the sake of our children. There is a reason God's love is compared to that of a mother. While God loves us more than we can ever hope to love our own children, there is no human love that compares with the love a mother has for her children.

QUESTIONS FOR REFLECTION

1. Why was it appropriate that the consequences of original sin for women be related to their roles as wife and mother?

2. How might pregnancy and postpartum life exacerbate women's body image issues?

3. How might we see our bodies in a more positive light during and after pregnancy?

4. How does the temptation to control and manipulate others negatively impact women's relationships with their husbands, other family members, friends, and coworkers?

5. How might using sex as leverage or bribery negatively impact a marriage?

An Exercise in Seeing Yourself as God Does

FOSTERING ACCEPTANCE WITH A BODY SCAN

In this chapter, we discussed how it can be difficult to accept our bodies as they change through our lives. Being able to be present to our bodies in the moment is a necessary step in acceptance. Consider using this exercise to help foster acceptance of your body as it is.

1. Find a quiet place to sit for about five to ten minutes.

2. Settle into a comfortable position. Take several deep breaths. Close your eyes.

3. Gently shift your attention to the top of your head. Begin to slowly scan down your body, forming a mental map of what you encounter. Pay attention to any physical sensations you observe: soreness, tension, relaxation, numbness. Just notice whatever sensations are present.

4. Notice any judgmental thoughts that arise, particularly as you scan areas of your body that cause you discomfort. Just allow them to flow in and out of awareness as you continue to scan your body.

5. As you scan your body and notice sensations, also notice
    if there is any underlying emotional quality present. If
    you are noticing tension, do you also notice anxiety? If
    your body feels heavy, do you notice sadness? Just allow
    yourself to consider any emotions present with curiosity.

6. As you finish your body scan, take a few deep breaths
    and notice how they feel in your body. Gently expand
    your awareness back out to the room around you and
    open your eyes.

7. Give thanks to God for a body that can feel all kinds
    of things.

Part 3

· · · · · · · · ·

YOU ARE
BLESSED

7

The Redemption of Man

I like to tell people that I'm a recovering perfectionist. I'm only half joking when I say it, but it always makes people laugh. Some people just think it's funny—why would you want to recover from being perfect, right? But other people know exactly what I'm talking about, and I can always tell by the half-hearted laugh they give me. They think the joke is cute, but the truth just hits a little too close to home for them. And I can totally understand their discomfort.

I have always been a perfectionist. I cried the first time I got a B+ at the end of a semester. I was a junior in college at the time, and I was devastated. During my years as a cheerleader, I spent hours practicing my routines until I had them down perfectly, which was quite impressive since I wasn't the most graceful girl to wear the uniform. Every morning during high school, I woke up with enough time to shower and fix my hair, even if it meant waking up at five a.m. to do it. I wanted to *be* perfect, and I hated that I wasn't. But I just kept on trying.

I assumed that if I wasn't perfect, people would love me less. I worried that if people realized I was faking it, they would decide that I wasn't worth the love they were giving me. I struggled to accept that anyone could love me with all my flaws. Over and over again, I projected my own fears and false beliefs onto other people. If I couldn't love myself as I was, how could anyone else? Why would they want to? I thought that if I was perfect (or if I made everyone think I was perfect), I would be worth more. I might finally be good enough. I craved perfection, and I couldn't wrap my head around the idea that God just wanted me to give my best, even if it wasn't perfect. How could my best ever be good enough if it wasn't perfect?

My perfectionism was a great asset in school, but it wreaked havoc on my mental health. Flaws could not be tolerated. Grades below a ninety were unacceptable. My clothes needed to be immaculate, my room needed to be pristine, and my life needed to be perfect. I demanded the same perfection for my body. I wanted my skin to be smooth and flawless. My hair needed to be silky and shiny. My body needed to have the perfect balance of curves and thinness. I wanted perfection, and I was willing to do anything to get it.

My unhealthy body image eventually led to an eating disorder. I never managed to reach perfection, but I told myself that good eating and exercise habits were essential if I was going to reach my goal. I needed to eat less and exercise more, and eventually I would be satisfied. But after ten years of striving for perfection, I realized I was chasing after an unrealistic goal. I was never going to be perfect, and I didn't need to be. I just needed to be the best I could be. My best would always be good enough for God. When I finally accepted that, I understood that I had always been enough. I had always striven to do my best, but now I didn't need to agonize over the gap between my best and perfection. My best was all I needed to give, and it was enough.

THE REDEMPTION OF THE BODY

Up until now, we have primarily focused on the story of Genesis, but that's only the first part of the story of mankind. The Bible is comprised of seventy-three books, with over a thousand chapters. Of those books, only one book describes the creation and fall of man, and even within that single book, the story of Creation and the Fall can be found in just the first three chapters. The rest of the Bible is the story of the redemption of man, which finds its completion, its consummation, at the cross of Christ. So this is what we will focus on from here on out.

Just as the fall of man ushered in two forms of death, Jesus Christ came to restore both forms of life to us. By joining divinity and humanity in one person, Jesus is capable of saving humanity. He can *save* us because he is God, but he can save *us* because he is human. By dying in his human flesh, Jesus conquers death, which cannot crush divinity and cannot conquer the perfect human man. By rising, Jesus restores life to humanity's fallen flesh. When Christ died on the cross, all mankind died with him. When he rose from the dead and came back to life, all mankind rose with him. As St. Paul tells us, "But if we have died with Christ, we believe that we shall also live with him" (Romans 6:8). When we unite ourselves with Christ, we participate in both his death and his resurrection.

Jesus Christ began the work of restoring his divine life to all mankind when he permitted his divinity to enter into human flesh. He redeemed all humanity through his actions, securing both physical and spiritual life for all those willing to accept it. He granted us all spiritual life by conquering death as one who is both fully God and fully man, and he promised us all physical life at his resurrection. Jesus' resurrection wasn't just spiritual, after all; it was physical. Jesus rose from the dead, body and soul. He has promised the same for us.

Through his resurrection, Christ invites us to consider our bodies in a new light—his light. If our bodies were just meaningless matter, he wouldn't have bothered to resurrect his own flesh. If our bodies didn't matter, he wouldn't have needed his own flesh when he rose from the dead. At the very least, he wouldn't have brought it with him to heaven. By ascending body and soul into heaven, Christ shows us that our bodies matter. Jesus Christ is true God and true man, and in order to be truly human, he needed his body. Our bodies are part of who we are, and we cannot be truly and fully ourselves without them. We wouldn't be truly and fully human without them.

THE GIFT OF FLESH AND BLOOD

Our bodies are gifts from God, flesh and blood lovingly crafted to be the revelation of our interior souls. They reveal who we are to the world. Our bodies were given to us so that we could fully experience the world around us through our senses. We can see, hear, smell, taste, and touch the world around us, the world that God gave us. The world is a gift designed to be experienced through the senses, so God gave us the sensitive flesh we needed to fully appreciate the beauty of everything he created.

If our bodies are gifts given to us by God, the best way to show our gratitude is by treating them with the respect and love they deserve. Our bodies are meant to be cherished and protected, to be nourished and adorned with care. When we eat well, exercise moderately, and dress with respect, we are showing God our gratitude. But when we starve ourselves, punish ourselves with exercise, and treat our bodies like objects, we are rejecting one of the greatest gifts we have ever been given.

When I really began to view my body as a gift from God to be treasured and respected, it changed everything for me. I couldn't starve myself without rejecting God's gift to me. I couldn't punish myself without ruining something that God really loved. Faced with the truth of God's love for all of me, including my body, as well as my own deep love for our Lord, I couldn't ignore the fact that when I critiqued and hated my body, I was critiquing and hating God. When I mistreated my body, I was mistreating God. When I belittled and disrespected my body, I was belittling and disrespecting God. I knew he didn't deserve to be treated like that, and neither did my body. I needed to abandon the lens of sin and learn how to see myself with the eyes of God. I needed to constantly remind myself that my body is a gift from God, and this flesh and blood that gives form to my soul, this body of mine, is the only body I will ever be given, and it is mine forever.

THE RESTORATION OF SPIRITUAL AND PHYSICAL LIFE

Jesus' death and resurrection redeemed all of us. He redeemed our entire humanity, which includes both our bodies and our souls. Just as Adam and Eve brought both physical and spiritual death upon all mankind, Jesus restores both physical and spiritual life. We are given spiritual life in Baptism, when we are washed clean of sin and remade into children of God. Without the stain of original sin, we are drawn into the family of God and become his adopted sons and daughters.

Christ's death and resurrection opened the doors of heaven to us, and in Baptism, we receive the promise of eternal life. We receive the Holy Spirit and are transformed into temples for the divine. Our *bodies* become temples of the Holy Spirit. As St. Paul tells us, "Do you not know that your body is a temple of the

Holy Spirit within you, which you have from God? You are not your own; you were bought with a price. So glorify God in your body" (1 Corinthians 6:19–20).

That's a pretty heavy truth. Our bodies are temples of the Holy Spirit. God dwells within us from the moment of our baptism. Once we have been baptized, the bond of communion between God and man is restored. We are cleansed in the waters of Baptism so that the divine can dwell in us. Man and God are once again united. But God is not finished with us. Baptism restores spiritual life to us, but it also bestows on us the promise of physical life. We believe in the saving waters of Baptism and the resurrection of the body. Our souls have been given spiritual life, but at the resurrection of the body, at the end of time, we will all receive our bodies back, and those who are saved will experience eternal glory.

That means that the body is here to stay. Our bodies are *ours* for the rest of eternity. The separation of body and soul that will occur at our deaths will not be permanent. Our bodies, the flesh that is currently ours, will be the bodies that are restored to us at the end of time. They will be different, but they will also be the same. As St. Paul writes in his first letter to the Corinthians:

> *What is sown is perishable, what is raised is imperishable. [The body] is sown in dishonor, it is raised in glory. It is sown in weakness, it is raised in power. It is sown a physical body, it is raised a spiritual body. If there is a physical body, there is also a spiritual body. Thus it is written, "The first man Adam became a living soul"; the last Adam became a life-giving spirit.*

Just as we have borne the image of the man of dust, we shall also bear the image of the man of heaven. (1 Corinthians 15:42–45, 49)

We were created as natural beings, condemned to death because of the stain of original sin on our souls. We were destined to die from before even our first breath. But in Baptism, we die in Christ and we rise in him, and just as Christ rose as a spiritual body made for eternal life, so too will we all experience eternal life in our bodies. When we rose up out of the waters of Baptism, this promise was extended to us. When we rise up out of our graves at the end of time, the promise Christ made to us will be fulfilled in our glorified bodies. The separation of body and soul is not the end for us. We will rise from the dead, just like Jesus Christ, who is called "the first-born of all creation" (Colossians 1:15). Christ has walked the path to eternal life first, but we are all called to follow after. He rose in his glorified flesh, and at the end of time, we hope to do the same. Christ shows us that we need our bodies to be fully human. We are enfleshed souls after all, and we cannot be fully ourselves without our own bodies and souls. They are *ours*. They make us *us*. We need them.

We are not destined to be disembodied souls for all eternity; we are destined to live forever as embodied souls possessing both an immortal soul and an immortal body. That is the vision God has for us. That was always his plan from the very beginning— to spend eternity with us. He will be our God, and we will be his people. His human people. His embodied people. That has always been his hope for us. But we are not ready yet. Our souls must be perfected first. Our bodies must be perfected first. That which is not perfect has no place in heaven.

THE CALL TO PERFECTION

Christ's call to perfection has always been a cross for me. I didn't understand it for a very long time. Christ calls us to "be perfect, as your heavenly Father is perfect" (Matthew 5:48). That seems like quite the extreme challenge. But it was exactly what I wanted. I thought it was proof that what I wanted and what God wanted was the same thing. I wanted to be perfect. He wanted me to be perfect. Perfect.

I justified my quest for perfection for years, telling myself that God wanted me to be perfect too. I needed to be as perfect as possible, which included perfect hair and skin, perfect grades and athletic performances, perfect presentations and recitals. I somehow managed to survive high school on just five hours of sleep a night, because I needed all those other hours to be perfect. I needed time to study and do homework, time to shower and style my hair, time to run and work out. I needed time to pray, but only when other people could see me, because I wanted people to see how perfect I was. But do you know what I didn't need time for? More than five hours of sleep a night. Eating well and at regular intervals. Spending time in private prayer in my room. My goal was perfection, and some things were much more important than others in my quest to finally be perfect.

But my definition of perfect and God's definition of perfect are so different. God doesn't care about perfect skin, perfect hair, or perfect clothes. He doesn't demand perfect grades, perfect performances, perfect works of art. When Jesus demands perfection, he is demanding moral perfection. He is calling us to be saints. We do not need to be flawless models to get into heaven; we need to be saints.

And if you really think about it, moral perfection, rather than physical perfection, makes perfect sense. If Jesus wants us to be perfect as our heavenly Father is perfect, he can't be talking about our bodies. God doesn't have a body, so he can't be telling us that our bodies must be perfect as our heavenly Father's body is perfect. God the Father is pure spirit; he doesn't have a body. So when Jesus calls us to perfection, he must be talking about something else.

There is a difference between being a perfectionist and working toward perfection. God calls us to perfection; he does not call us to be perfectionists. He asks that we give our all, our everything, our best, but he does not ask for what we do not have. He wants saints, not perfectionists. When we do our best, when we choose to act in a saintly fashion, we are answering Jesus' call to perfection. But we are answering it as fallen (and redeemed) human beings. The road to perfection will not be easy. It is not always pretty. We will fall. We will scrape our knees and scratch our elbows. We will pour out blood, sweat, and tears. But we will get up again. We will allow ourselves to be lifted when we can't lift ourselves. We will walk the way of the cross.

THE SALVATION OF THE WORLD

When Christ died on the cross, he didn't just redeem mankind. He saved the world. He is the true Superman. When Adam and Eve fell in the Garden, they took the whole world down with them. When Christ rose from the dead, he brought the entire world back up. Christ is not just our Savior; he is the Savior of the world.

Obviously, Christ's redemption of the world does not negate the fact that the world fell in the first place. The same goes for us. Even though we have been saved, we are still capable of sin. The consequences of the Fall are still in effect. We still die. Women still suffer in childbirth. Men still struggle against the earth to provide for their families. The world still works against us. But the world is not evil. It is fallen, but it's not evil.

Even though we are fallen creatures living in a fallen world, the original call of God remains. When God created Adam and Eve, he commanded them to "fill the earth and subdue it" and to "have dominion" (Genesis 1:28). Mankind was given the task of caring for the earth. We were meant to be its stewards. The earth was entrusted to us for safekeeping, but we are also invited to use it.

We are not supposed to control the world, but we are also not meant to be controlled by it. We are supposed to use it and care for it. We are meant to enjoy it. The world is good, and it was given to us as a good to be enjoyed, and despite its fallen nature, the world's innate goodness continues to exist. We might be tempted to abuse this world and to abuse ourselves by allowing created things to control us, but this world is still good.

And it wasn't just created good before it was irrevocably destroyed by man's sin; the world has been redeemed as well. God's grace flows through all of his creation. In the sacraments, water can remove sin. Bread and wine can become the Body, Blood, Soul, and Divinity of Jesus Christ. Blessed oil (chrism) can mark us with the Holy Spirit. Creation is filled with grace, and when we recognize the world for what it is, God's grace can flow. When we open ourselves to God's grace and participate in the sacraments, we can stop going to war with the world. We can actually enjoy the world. We can appreciate the world for what it is, a gift from God.

LIVING AS A RECOVERING PERFECTIONIST

I spent more than a decade trying to make my body perfect. I binged and purged regularly. I over-exercised on a daily basis.

I threw out an embarrassing amount of food. I spent hours agonizing over every unwanted pound, every frayed hair, every blemish on my face. I chased after perfection desperately, but I never caught it. And now? I'm glad that I didn't. I never needed to be perfect. The bodily perfection I longed for was not the type of perfection God wanted for me.

God never wanted me to be perfect, not the way that I wanted to be perfect, at least. He wants me to be the best I can be. He wants me to do my best, to give my all, to recognize when I need help, and to entrust everything else to God. As the saying goes, "Work as if everything depends on you; pray as if everything depends on God." I spent years trying to span the bridge between my best and absolute perfection, but now I know the truth. I could never cross that bridge myself. It has never been within my abilities to do so. God was the only Person who could cross that divide. His grace has made my best sufficient. My best is enough for God, so it should be enough for me too.

I'm striving for a different type of perfection now. I'm still chasing after perfection, but at least now I have an attainable goal: heaven. God wants me to become a saint. He doesn't care how much I weigh as I do it. Restricting food and over-exercising are not going to get me into heaven faster. St. Peter is not going to turn me away at the pearly gates because I still had that last five pounds to lose when I died. None of that will matter in the end. I will not be judged on how I look. I will be judged on how I lived.

There is no special place in heaven for women with impeccable hair, flawless skin, and perfect bodies. You don't get extra points on Judgment Day if you "bounced back" quickly after being pregnant, or if you straightened your hair every single morning before you left the house. Yes, our bodies matter and how we treat our bodies matters, but perfect hair and skin won't matter.

God considers how we use the gifts he has given us, including our bodies, but he is not counting how many salads we've eaten or how many workouts we have logged. That's not the kind of stuff that God is keeping track of for our day of judgment.

Our judgment will be about how we have lived. It will be about how we used our bodies. It will be about how we have loved and given ourselves to others. Spending your entire life chasing after "perfection" won't get you to heaven any faster. If anything, it might have you running in the wrong direction. I'm running a different race now, and my new finish line is a much more worthwhile goal. When I stand before God for judgment, I hope to say with St. Paul, "I have fought the good fight, I have finished the race, I have kept the faith" (2 Timothy 4:7). That is the only prize worth winning, and I hope you'll join me in running the race. It's a marathon we are all running, and as any runner knows, a marathon is easier to run when we have friends running alongside us.

QUESTIONS FOR REFLECTION

1. Have you ever struggled with the need to be perfect? What is the difference between perfectionism and the desire to give our best?

2. What is the significance of Christ's bodily resurrection when it comes to how we view our own bodies?

3. What is the difference between Christ's call to perfection in the Gospel and our tendency to perfectionism?

4. What does it mean to be stewards of the world God has given us? How can we be better stewards of the bodies God has given us?

5. How might you better strive for God's perfection in your daily life?

An Exercise in Seeing Yourself as God Does

BE A COMPASSIONATE FRIEND

Many of us attempt to control every aspect of our lives in the hope that it will bring us a sense of peace and belonging. While it can be tempting to believe harsh self-criticism will drive us forward toward perfection and, therefore, the life we seek, that often acts as a stumbling block to true peace. Instead, meeting ourselves with compassion when we fall short of our goals allows us to meet inevitable failures with a gentleness that makes it more likely we will get up and try again. It is important to understand what is meant by self-compassion in this context. Self-compassion is not weakness or laziness. It is not approval of all behaviors and a loss of standards. Instead, self-compassion is meeting the sufferings and challenges in our lives with kindness and gentleness. Self-compassion guides us to meet our failures with warmth and encouragement to try again. It can be difficult to immediately shift from self-criticism to self-compassion. Consider using this exercise to begin practicing self-compassion:

1. Find a quiet place to sit for a few minutes. Ask God to allow you to see with compassionate eyes during this exercise.

2. Begin by taking a few deep breaths. Allow yourself to come into the present moment.

3. Call to mind a recent experience where you failed to live up to the standards you set for yourself. Notice any thoughts and emotions that arise as you recall this experience. Allow them to be present without judgment.

4. Now step outside of yourself in this memory and imagine instead that it is your friend who has fallen short of their goals or standards. How do you imagine they would feel? What might they be thinking? Allow yourself to feel empathy and compassion for them.

5. Now consider how you might speak to this friend who is suffering. Would you yell at them? Tell them how stupid they are? Criticize them for being a failure? Or would you speak gently to them? Acknowledge that it is painful to fall short of our goals? Encourage them to try again?

6. Allow yourself to notice how you are feeling as you offer compassionate encouragement to your friend. Consider how this compares with how you speak to yourself in difficult moments.

7. Finish this exercise by taking a few deep breaths. Return your awareness to the room around you. Offer gratitude to God for anything you noticed in this exercise. Open your eyes.

8

The Body Redeemed and Restored

Our bodies are capable of telling an incredible story. Before we even say a word, our bodies can communicate so much about us to other people. In my thirty-plus years of life, I have gained many wounds and earned many scars. I have a faint line beneath my chin where my tooth tore through the skin after I fell at the playground. (Ironically, my son has the same scar in the same place from the same type of fall.) I have two very visible scars on my left arm from multiple surgeries after a bicycle accident. For a while, I was seeing a chiropractor on a monthly basis to deal with a hip injury that was aggravated after giving birth. Our bodies are covered in marks that tell our stories.

In the weeks and months that followed the surgeries for my arm, I tried to hide the scars as much as possible. I opted for long-sleeved shirts when I could wear them and worked to keep my hand gesturing to a minimum (which was difficult for a girl with Italian roots). Eventually, I realized people didn't care about the scars. My friends were still my friends. Acquaintances remained acquaintances. As I got older, my scars even became an asset from time to time. It was a convenient topic of conversation among both friends and strangers, and during the years in ministry work, my students thought my scars were awesome. They only added to my popularity among the children.

It took me several years, but I eventually realized that I didn't need to be ashamed of my scars. I didn't need to be embarrassed. Yes, the wounds had caused me pain, but the scars that remained were just part of my story. My chin scar is proof that despite years of figure skating and cheerleading, I am still a bit of a klutz. My arm scars are pretty much proof of the same, since they are evidence that I can make just sitting on a bicycle dangerous. And my bad hip is a regular reminder that I have brought two incredible children into this world. Those marks, and the countless others that adorn my body, are all part of my story, the story of my life. And they are also a reminder that my story is not finished.

BORN OF WATER AND THE SPIRIT

My two children were baptized at one month and three weeks, respectively. Both of their baptisms were scheduled months in advance, and we had godparents chosen for both of our children before they were even conceived. Their baptismal garments were purchased and hanging in their closets before they were even brought home from the hospital. Having our children baptized was obviously a high priority for us.

I love looking back at pictures of my children's baptisms. They were so tiny when they were presented to the Church as her newest members. We had picked out adorable baptismal garments for them, but they were both so tiny that they were easily lost in all the extra fabric. They slept through most of the ceremony and reception, enjoying the blissful sleep of the innocent. And they were so innocent. So pure. So perfect.

Our baptism marks the beginning of our spiritual lives. In a very real sense, we are all born dead. Stained by the mark of original sin, we are doomed to death from the moment of our conception. We are born separated from God, even if he remains the cause of our very existence. We can't live with him (in heaven), but we can't live without him. We need him. God gives us physical life at our conception, but he gives us spiritual life at our baptism. And he's not finished there. He still has more in mind for us.

Baptism is just the starting point for reestablishing unity between our bodies and souls. Baptism bestows on us spiritual life but also the promise of eternal life with God. We become spiritually alive at our baptism, but we will still die one day. The difference is that Baptism opens the gates of heaven for us. This is why we drape a white pall over coffins and light the Paschal candle during funerals. Our deaths are another birth or, to be more precise, the fulfillment of that rebirth established at Baptism. But that's not the end either.

Baptism gives us spiritual life and the promise of supernatural physical life at the resurrection of the body. God doesn't intend us to spend eternity bodiless. We were created as embodied spirits, and that is how we are meant to live. Death might bring about the separation of our bodies and souls, but even as we live, our bodies and souls are being prepared for eternal life. In the sacraments, our bodies and souls are transformed. In Baptism, we become children of God and heirs to the kingdom of heaven. In Confirmation, our bodies become temples of the Holy Spirit. In the Eucharist, we become more fully members of the Body of Christ as his Body becomes united with our bodies. The sacraments all serve as confirmation that our bodies really matter.

When we receive the Eucharist, we receive Christ into our bodies. We receive his Body into our bodies, and the two bodies become one flesh. We are fully united to Christ. He is in us. When we love our bodies, we are loving God in our bodies. When we respect our bodies and treat them properly, we are respecting God in our bodies. But when we mistreat our bodies and hate our bodies, we are betraying God's love and denying him in our flesh. But God is merciful. He offers us forgiveness in so many ways because he wants us to learn to love our bodies as he does.

LAYING DOWN OUR BURDENS AND CARRYING OUR CROSSES

Even with the graces of Baptism, we are not impervious to sin. We might have been freed from original sin and forgiven of all our actual sin, but we are not freed from the temptation to sin. Christ has redeemed us, but we remain fallen creatures. We are still plagued by sin. Choosing Christ does not make us immune to temptation. Being baptized does not create a shield to protect us from sin. Instead, Baptism gives us the grace to withstand temptation and to persevere when we fall. Choosing Christ means accepting our crosses, as well as accepting whatever help God gives us to endure. Jesus has promised us eternal life in heaven, not a cakewalk while we are here on earth.

Christ invited us to lay down our burdens, but he also called us to take up our crosses and follow him. So what does that mean for us? It means that our lives won't always be easy. We will suffer. We will struggle. We will trip and fall and lack the strength to stand back up on our own. But it also means that we can unite our crosses with the cross of Christ. He can make our suffering worthwhile. He can make our struggles redemptive. If we trust in Christ, he will give us the grace to carry our crosses, and that grace can take a myriad of forms.

Sometimes God gives us the strength and perseverance we need to carry our crosses throughout our entire lives. Sometimes he gives us a reprieve from our struggles in the form of a miracle. And sometimes God gives us a Simon of Cyrene to carry our crosses with us when they get too heavy. God's grace is always sufficient, but it doesn't always take the form we expect or even want. But God never promised that our lives would be easy if we repented and believed in him. He only promised that his grace would be enough. And God does not break his promises.

I have carried many different crosses in my life. The two biggest ones were my ten-year struggle with an eating disorder and my current struggle with secondary infertility. In the case of the first cross, I spent nearly the entire time I carried it pretending that it didn't exist. Even as it bore down on my soul and its burden became more and more oppressive, I refused to admit that I was suffering under its weight. And then it was just gone. I didn't even notice its absence at first. Overwhelmed with the reality that I was newly employed, newly married, and newly pregnant, I didn't even notice when the cross disappeared.

I do remember the moment that I realized it was gone, though. I was about four months postpartum, alone with my son for the evening, and when I normally would have been tempted to binge on snack foods *just because*, I found myself standing in front of our kitchen cupboards debating whether or not I was really hungry. And in that moment, I was struck by the truth. Throughout the entire length of my eating disorder, deciding whether or not I was hungry had never been a factor when thinking about food. Eating was occasionally about sustenance, but it was mostly about feeling better. It was about feeling full when I felt so empty inside. It was about feeling light when my body just felt too heavy of a burden to carry. It was about feeling momentarily happy when my life made me feel sad. It was about feeling temporarily satisfied when my life left me wondering if there was more out there that I was missing. But as I stared into our kitchen cupboards, I realized that I was finally freed from the burden of that cross. I no longer saw food as the enemy. And then I closed the cabinet door and returned to my TV show, empty-handed. I wasn't really hungry, so I wasn't going to eat. It seems so simple an idea—not eating when you're not hungry—but for me, after ten years of struggling with an eating disorder—it was pure joy. I finally felt free.

We create some of the crosses we carry ourselves. The vices we acquire as the result of repeated bad choices are heavy burdens that God never wanted us to carry. They are crosses that we are called to put down at the feet of Christ, to reject in favor of a life of virtue. They are crosses that we are meant to give to Christ so that he can cast them far away from us. As Jesus himself tells us, "Come to me, all who labor and are heavy laden, and I will give you rest. Take my yoke upon you, and learn from me; for I am gentle and lowly in heart, and you will find rest for your souls. For my yoke is easy, and my burden is light" (Matthew 11:28–30). The burden of an eating disorder is not the type of cross that Jesus tells us to carry when we follow him. It's a yoke that has been placed on us through the Devil's temptations and our own sinfulness.

Other crosses are more complicated. They are put on our shoulders through no fault of our own, just as the cross of Calvary was placed on Jesus' shoulders despite the fact that he had done nothing wrong. Most of us will carry crosses like this at some point in our lives, or for our entire lives. Illness, injuries, infertility, and the loss of loved ones—these are all crosses that we carry. These crosses can be treated as burdens that weigh us down and lead us to despair, or we can choose to unite our crosses to the cross of Christ, joining our suffering with that of Christ at Calvary.

This is what St. Paul is talking about when he writes to the Colossians, "Now I rejoice in my sufferings for your sake, and in my flesh I complete what is lacking in Christ's afflictions for the sake of his body, that is, the Church" (Colossians 1:24). Christ's suffering did not lack anything. He carried the suffering of all mankind in his body as it hung on the cross. He carried the weight of the sins of all mankind when he was crucified. In a very real sense, there couldn't have been anything lacking in the suffering of Christ. He carried it all. So what does St. Paul mean? He means that while there is nothing that Christ could add to his suffering on the cross, we can still add ourselves. We are members of his Body. When we are baptized in Christ, we are crucified with him. As we plunge into the waters of Baptism, we die with him. And then, as we rise up out of those same waters, symbolic of the grave, we rise to new life with him. Christ can add nothing to his cross because he has already given all of himself, but as members of his Body, baptized into his crucifixion and resurrection, we can add ourselves. Our bodies can spiritually be crucified with his. Our cross becomes his, and he carries it with us. We are what's lacking in Christ's afflictions—our own afflictions, which are united to his own since we are all members of his Body. And when we unite our crosses with his, they cease to be burdens that are too heavy to carry. Christ carries our crosses with us and for us.

My own struggle with secondary infertility is one such cross. We did not struggle to conceive our first two children, but since then, we have had no success in becoming pregnant. For nearly three years now, we have diligently charted in the hopes of conceiving. I have met with doctors and undergone testing, but we are still no closer to figuring out why we cannot conceive than we were three years ago when we began. It is a cross that my husband and I never imagined carrying, and yet here we are, carrying it nonetheless. In the beginning, I felt oppressed by the weight of the cross and overburdened with countless doctor appointments and blood draws. Our desperate attempts to get pregnant wreaked havoc on our emotional and spiritual health, our relationships, and our marriage. We felt lost and unsure of what God had planned for our life and our family.

But then God spoke to us through the wise words of one of his priests, who told us that while infertility is one of the heaviest crosses a married couple might be asked to carry, the heavier the cross, the more abundant the graces that can flow from it. The cross of infertility can be an overflowing fount of grace, but we must offer it to Christ to be transformed. We cannot cling to it, languishing in despair and comfortable beneath its familiar weight. We must hand over our burdens to Christ, offering our cross as a sacrifice to God to do with it what he will. Jesus Christ's crucifixion was a channel of immense grace. Through his suffering and death, he saved the world. Now we, as baptized members of his Body, are invited to offer up our own crosses so that they might be transformed into channels of grace. Once my husband and I handed over the cross of our infertility, the graces became apparent. We have become more aware of the hand of God in our own family life, and we have become conduits of grace to our family and friends. Our cross still feels heavy at times, but more than anything else, we find Christ in our suffering. Our suffering has meaning. Christ has redeemed man's suffering, and now our suffering, when it is united with Christ's own suffering and transformed into a source of grace, can be redemptive as well.

CARRYING THE INVISIBLE CROSS

All of us will carry a cross at some point in our lives. As Christians, we are meant to follow in the footsteps of Christ, and he walked the road to Calvary with a cross weighing him down. That is the path that we all must walk. We all must carry our crosses, bearing their weight on a daily basis. Our crosses are all different. Some of our crosses are obvious, while others are invisible. Some of us have endured poverty, illness, and the deaths of loved ones. Some of our crosses are bared for the world to see. But some of us carry invisible crosses, like struggles with mental health. All of our crosses are heavy and cumbersome, but these invisible crosses carry a weight all their own. It's especially difficult to carry a cross that no one else can see.

Struggles with self-image and mental illness are invisible crosses that many of us women carry on a daily basis. Women with eating disorders, depression, and anxiety often suffer in silence and in secret. Keeping our struggles a secret is often just part of the illness. Many of us are seeking "perfection" in ways that on some deep level we know are unhealthy, but to admit that we are sick is to admit that we are not perfect. And to admit that we are not perfect is to admit that we have failed, that we are not good enough, that we are not strong enough. Admitting to our struggles requires that we open up, and after living with our secrets for so long, that's a hard thing to do.

Many of us falsely believe that our faith will chase our illness away. We assume that if we pray hard enough, God will take away our suffering. But Christianity does not promise a struggle-free life. It simply ensures that our suffering has meaning. We can unite our crosses with the cross of Christ. We can unite our suffering with his. Just as he offered up his suffering for the world, we can offer up our struggles for those we love. We can turn our suffering into a sacrifice, offered on behalf of those who need or want our prayers.

Our struggles with mental illness and poor self-image can be redemptive. They can mean something. They don't need to be simply burdens. Christ invites us to lay our burdens down at his feet after all, not necessarily so that he can take them away but so that he can transform them. Jesus can take our struggles and give them meaning. No one wants to suffer, but more than that, no one wants to suffer unnecessarily. No one wants his or her struggles to mean nothing. Jesus Christ invites us to offer up our suffering on behalf of others. Suffering is inevitable, so we might as well have that suffering serve a purpose. The burden becomes easier to bear when it has meaning. We might not want to suffer, but at least it can be meaningful when it has been united to the cross of Christ.

BEARING OUR MARKS WITH GRACE

My body is riddled with small scars from skating accidents, bike mishaps, and a whole variety of clumsy moments. My skin has been stretched taut over widened hips and a bulging belly in pregnancy, and my body has accommodated a growing child not once but twice. I have created permanent laugh lines from years of regular occasions of joy, and my children have created permanent bags under my eyes from years of nighttime feedings, illnesses, and early morning bathroom trips. My body has been scarred over the years, but my inner scars have been so much more damaging than my physical ones.

My inner scarring is the reason why I care about my outward scars so much. If I hadn't been so wounded on the inside, my outside wounds wouldn't be such a problem. I wouldn't care about my scars so much. Healing is a slow process, but over the years, I've come to realize that many of my scars should be marks of pride for me. I earned those scars. My blood, sweat, and tears went into getting some of the scars. I should not be ashamed of them.

Many of my scars will not survive the separation of my body and soul at my death. When my body is resurrected at the Second Coming, most of my scars will be gone. Falling on the playground did not impact my salvation. I probably didn't lose time in Purgatory because of the bike accident that resulted in two surgeries and weeks of physical therapy. But I wouldn't be surprised if some of my "scars" are here to stay.

When Christ rose from the dead, his resurrected body was undeniably different. The disciple Mary Magdalene didn't even recognize him when she first saw him. The disciples on the road to Emmaus didn't recognize him either. Christ's body was different, but it was still undeniably his. He even bore the wounds of his crucifixion. That's right—his resurrected, glorified body has *scars*. These scars might seem like imperfections on his otherwise flawless skin, but they are not. Christ's wounds are proof of his salvific actions on the cross. His pierced hands, feet, and side are all signs of our redemption. They are not flaws; they are signs of hope. They are marks of our salvation.

Christ bears the wounds of his crucifixion, even after rising from the dead. Traditionally, the martyrs are depicted with the marks of their death as well, presumably because they will also bear these scars at the resurrection of the body at the end of time. Not all scars are imperfections. Some scars are a testimony to our faith. Some scars bear witness to the love we have for God and our fellow man. Some wounds and scars are meant to be glorious.

Will we bear some of the scars we have gained during our time here on earth on our resurrected bodies? Maybe. Maybe not. Most scars will surely fade. My resurrected body won't need to bear witness to the fact that I couldn't play without slicing my chin open or scraping my knee. It won't need to serve as a reminder of the two surgeries required to fix my broken arm. But not all scars are imperfections. Are the marks of my motherhood here to stay? Perhaps. I have found Christ in my vocation as wife and mother. I would not be at all surprised if some of the physical marks of my motherhood remain, even after I have been resurrected. I can't be certain, but I do know that if we do bear such "scars," we will not be ashamed of them.

LETTING GO OF SHAME

I have known what it feels like to be ashamed. I've tried to hide my scars countless times. I thought they were proof that I was broken, but over time my opinion of my scars has changed. Yes, some of my scars are evidence of breaking, but they are also proof of healing. Some scars might be imperfections on my skin, but they don't make me any less perfect. They don't change how God sees me, or how he loves me. He doesn't see those scars as defects. He sees how strong I've been and how I've struggled and overcome.

And some scars aren't scars at all. Some scars are meant to be badges of honor, evidence that God chose me to be the mother of some of his beloved children. Some marks make me even more beautiful, because they bear witness to the miracles I have born within my body. I should not be ashamed of those marks. I should be grateful. I should be proud. My body is my story made present, and my body is a story of love—the love of husband and wife for their little girl, the love of a man for his wife, the love of a mother for her children, and the love of God for his beautiful daughter.

QUESTIONS FOR REFLECTION

1. Why should Christ's indwelling in us affect the way we consider and treat our bodies?

2. How does Christ's suffering and death revolutionize our own struggles?

3. What is the value in considering our suffering to be redemptive?

4. Why would Jesus Christ continue to bear the scars of his crucifixion even after his resurrection?

5. What are the some of the marks that you bear on your body? How can they be transformed from shameful scars into badges of honor?

An Exercise in Seeing Yourself as God Does

SUFFERING IN THE SERVICE OF WHAT?

In this chapter, we discussed the importance of taking up our crosses and following Christ. In taking up our crosses, we do not avoid suffering. Instead, taking up our crosses in faith and trust ensures that our suffering has meaning and our lives have purpose. Throughout the previous exercises, we have discussed ways to contact and allow different aspects of suffering, like uncomfortable thoughts and painful feelings. But why should we seek to accept and be present to these discomforts? We seek to embrace these discomforts because they are part of the cross, and if we do not embrace them, we cannot step out fully into the lives our Lord has planned for us.

The things that give meaning and purpose to our lives are sometimes called values. Values are not discrete tasks that can be crossed off a list like a goal. They act more like a compass. While a compass may help guide you north, you never "reach north" and check it off the list. Similarly, values help you choose behaviors as you move through life in a way that gives life meaning. As Catholics, we know broadly that our primary value is to love God and love one another. It can be helpful to get clarity about the ways you are called to do that individually and in different domains of your life. Consider how you might live out the Christian call to love in the following domains of your life. Be specific about what behaviors you would engage in if you were fully living a life of love.

- family

- friendships

- work/school

- health

- community life (e.g., parish)

- spiritual life (e.g., personal prayer)

- add any additional domains that are meaningful to you

9

The Great Gift of Motherhood

Before my husband and I started our family, I assumed that I would only have girls. I just couldn't imagine raising boys, but then I had my son, and now I have the great pleasure of having both a son and a daughter. Already at the ages of six and four, the differences between the sexes are obvious. My son loves fighting and playing war games. He is obsessed with dinosaurs and superheroes. And then there's my daughter. I swear she has had a swagger to her step since the day she learned to walk. She swings her hips and plants her hands on her waist just like a little woman. At the age of three and a half, she is already sassy, sweet, and so, so beautiful.

My children are still young, but I'm already thinking about how the world will treat them as they get older. Modern media doesn't exactly provide good role models for our children, and I'm worried that today's TV shows and movies will teach lessons to my children that are not healthy for them. Most of the men in today's TV shows and movies are dim-witted, weak, and incompetent. The women, on the other hand, are power hungry, selfish, and frankly a little too manly for my tastes. I don't want my son to think he's weak, and I don't want my daughter to think she needs to do everything on her own. I want more for my children.

I'm afraid that one day the world will break my beautiful daughter's fragile heart. I'm afraid that she will believe the world's lies. I'm afraid that she will think she is not pretty enough, not thin enough, not strong enough. I want her to know that she is beautiful. I want her to know that she has been fearfully and wonderfully made. I want her to know that she is enough, perfect just the way she is. My daughter is God's perfect masterpiece, and my husband and I are both so in love with her.

MARY, THE NEW EVE

Mary is called the new, or second, Eve (see CCC 511). Where Eve fell, Mary has been exalted. Both came into being without original sin, but one chose herself while the other chose God. Where Eve chose to abandon God, Mary chose to receive God within her, giving birth to the Son of God. Mary actually got to experience God growing inside her. Even though it is Eve whose name means "mother of all the living," it is Mary who became the mother of Life himself.

Mary and Eve both experienced pregnancy and childbirth, but they had very different experiences. Eve, having already fallen, experienced the consequences of sin as she became a mother. She experienced her pregnancy as a woman already cursed by sin and death. Her body rebelled against her, and as Cain grew within her womb, her body resisted the growing life inside her. She could have experienced all the negative side effects of pregnancy, from morning sickness to swollen ankles and joint pain. And nothing could have prepared her for the pain of childbirth, since she was the first woman to experience it.

Mary, on the other hand, is the first woman to experience pregnancy and childbirth as all women were meant to experience it. Possessing a body and soul perfectly in communion with one another, Mary suffered none of the characteristics of pregnancy brought on by the Fall. Her labor was painless, and her delivery was smooth and quick. Her body did exactly what it was meant to do. She had the experience intended for all women, including you, me, and Eve.

Mary is proof that biological motherhood was always part of God's plan for women. Her experience of pregnancy and childbirth shows us something of that original plan. Her skin stretched to accommodate her baby boy, but she experienced no ligament pains. She gained weight as her son grew, but she never could have failed her glucose test (not that she was given one). She gave birth to a healthy baby boy, but she did so without tearing and as a virgin.[8] Her breasts filled with milk so that Christ could nurse, but she never suffered from mastitis. Mary experienced all the beauty of pregnancy and childbirth but none of the pains.

Did Mary have stretch marks? Perhaps. Did she gain weight? Certainly. Did her breasts become heavy with milk? Naturally, so that she might feed her son. Did her back ache and ankles swell from the extra weight she carried? Maybe, but maybe not. Did her labor and delivery scar her at all? Definitely not. She bore no true scars from her experience of childbirth, but she certainly bore the marks of her motherhood upon her flesh. Those marks are beautiful though, and never once did she consider being ashamed of them. Conceived without sin and having never sinned

---

8   Church teaching asserts that Mary was a virgin before, during, and after the birth of Christ. While we know what it means for her to have been a virgin before and after birth, theologians can only speculate at what it might mean for Mary to have been a virgin during birth. This is one aspect of childbirth that does set Mary aside from the rest of women. Hers is the only virgin birth in history.

herself, Mary had the full, perfect experience of what it means to be a mother.

MARY, MOTHER OF THE CHURCH

Mary has also experienced spiritual motherhood. She didn't just give birth to Jesus Christ in Bethlehem. She also gave birth to the Church at the foot of the cross. When Jesus gave his beloved disciple John to his mother, he was entrusting all people to Mary. She is not just the mother of Christ. She is the mother of the Church. She is our Mother. Mary is Jesus' biological mother, but she is the spiritual mother of all Christians. God made Mary, like Eve before her, mother of all the living.

In the book of Revelation, John sees the following vision:

> And a great sign appeared in heaven, a woman clothed with the sun, with the moon under her feet, and on her head a crown of twelve stars; she was with child and she cried out in her pangs of birth, in anguish for delivery. (Revelation 12:1–2)

Mary is not only the perfect role model for physical motherhood. She is also the perfect role model for spiritual motherhood. At the foot of the cross, Mary received all people as her spiritual sons and daughters. She willingly accepted each and every one of us as her children, baggage and all. She loves us as only a mother can. Her mother's heart is wide enough to encompass all of us, and it is always expanding.

Mary is proof that motherhood is not merely biological. It goes so far beyond the simple ability to carry and bring children into the world. Spiritual motherhood is not easy, just as physical motherhood can be difficult at times. There is a reason why Mary groans in pain as she gives birth to the Church. Mary did not suffer when she gave birth to the Son of God, but she certainly suffered to give birth to the Church. Mary watched her beloved son as he died, and as blood and water poured from the side of Christ, Mary celebrated the birth of the Church even as she mourned the suffering and death of her son. Even as she lost her own son to death, Mary accepted her role as the mother of the Church. Jesus did not leave her empty-handed, and now Mary's arms are always filled with new beloved sons and daughters.

CO-CREATORS WITH GOD

Mary cooperated with God in order to usher in salvation. She said yes at the annunciation, allowing herself to be overshadowed by the Holy Spirit so that she could become the Mother of God. She said yes at the wedding feast at Cana, knowing that Christ's public ministry would end in his death. She said yes at the cross, handing her son over to the Father even as she accepted into her empty arms the lives of all God's children. She said yes to her motherhood so many times. We are called to do the same.

Husbands and wives are invited to become co-creators with God whenever they come together in the marital act. When they open themselves up to the possibility of children, they cooperate with God to bring about new life. God created Adam and Eve from the dust, but the nature of their creation is unique. The rest of us, Mary and Jesus included, are born of a woman. God does not create human lives without us. He has invited us to participate in this incredible miracle, and women get to experience this gift in a very physical way.

Mothers have the unique opportunity to feel that new life grow within them. Where there once was emptiness, now there is a fullness that cannot be described. To have your children grow larger, to feel them hiccup, to see their head and limbs move just below your skin—the feeling cannot be explained in words. It can only be experienced, and we women have been given the great gift to be the ones to feel it. We get to experience the miracle of life, a miracle that we had a hand in bringing about, in our very bodies.

Procreation allows us to cooperate with God, creating life with him. It allows us to be like God. We can participate in God's creative work. By offering ourselves and our marriages to God, we can become like him. But God didn't just create us. He also suffered for us. He sacrificed his body for us. He gave his life for us. When we become co-creators with God, our offering is lifelong. Our offering demands that we give everything, that we give all of ourselves. And for us women, that offering often takes a very literal, physical form. We will suffer for our children. We will sacrifice our bodies. We might even give up our lives for them.

With each pregnancy, we give our bodies to our children. For nine months, they grow inside of us, stretching our skin and shifting our organs. Our bodies become foreign to us as our children make them their homes. Even after they are born, our children continue to use our bodies. They nurse at our breasts. They find rest in our arms. They fall asleep in our laps. Our bodies support them, shelter them, and offer them comfort. Our bodies are ours as much as they are theirs.

And the sacrifice is not limited to biological mothers. Teachers give up their sleep and unpaid time preparing classrooms and lesson plans, grading schoolwork, and agonizing over the well-being of their students. Godparents, foster parents, and adoptive parents love their children with the same type of consuming, exhausting love with which biological parents love their children. They hold them, rock them, worry over them, just as any mother would over her children. They have given their bodies to their children as only women know how.

REDEMPTIVE MOTHERHOOD

With Mary's *fiat* at the annunciation, motherhood was drawn into God's plan of salvation. Jesus Christ, with the cooperation of his mother, used motherhood as the initial vehicle for man's redemption. Mankind was punished for its original sin in ways that touched at the core of who they were as men and women, but Jesus Christ redeemed those same experiences in his birth, life, death, and resurrection. Adam's punishment for his original sin had been toil and struggle to provide for his loved ones. The new Adam, Jesus Christ, redeemed man's toil by going about his Father's work during his life and then shedding blood, tears, and sweat during his passion and death. Similarly, Eve's punishment for her original sin had been pain and suffering in childbirth, but Jesus Christ redeemed that experience when he permitted himself to be born of a woman. Mary, the new Eve, ushered in man's salvation through her pregnancy, and as a result, motherhood has been redeemed and transformed to become a vehicle of redemption for all women.

Jesus Christ redeemed all mankind through his life, death, and resurrection. It is through him that we are all saved, but like Mary, we are called to cooperate with God in our salvation. St. Paul wrote in his letter to the Philippians that we all must "work out [our] own salvation with fear and trembling" (Philippians 2:12). Christ paid our debt in full with his death and resurrection, but we are still required to accept that payment with our very lives. We are saved when we are baptized, but even the baptized can fall into mortal sin. Salvation is an ongoing process on our part, lived out from the day we are baptized until the day we die. Our salvation was won for us, but it can also be lost. Our cooperation, our faith and works, are the way that we give our own *fiat* to the work of redemption in our lives. And for women, this can and often does include childbirth.

Motherhood, both in a spiritual and physical sense, is woman's road to salvation. Mary and Jesus transformed pregnancy and childbirth in this fallen, but redeemed, world. The punishment for our sin has in fact become the path to our salvation. St. Paul asserts as much when he writes to Timothy that "woman will be saved through bearing children, if she continues in faith and love and holiness, with modesty" (1 Timothy 2:15). The suffering we endure during pregnancy and childbirth can be offered up for our own salvation and for the sins of others. The hours and energy that we offer the children we love, whether they are biologically ours or not, can be offered up as well. We can make our bodies a gift that is offered to God as a sacrifice for our own redemption. We can embrace our transformed bodies as the very instruments of our salvation. Motherhood allows us to imitate Christ more fully, giving our bodies to our children just as Jesus gave up his body for us. Redemptive motherhood gives a whole new meaning to our bodies.

This is only possible because Jesus Christ has redeemed not only motherhood but also suffering. We as baptized Christians are invited to unite our suffering with that of Jesus on the Cross, transforming it into a sacrifice of love for our own needs as well as the needs of others. Jesus Christ paid the price for our salvation in his body, and we, as members of his Mystical Body, are called to do the same. We pay the price in our own bodies whenever we choose to unite ourselves with Christ. We suffer with him, we sacrifice ourselves in him, and we are saved through him. By uniting our suffering with that of Jesus Christ, we cooperate in the work of our salvation, being redeemed through pregnancy and childbirth.

RAISING THE NEXT GENERATION OF WOMEN

I gave my body to my children. Now I hope to spare them from the struggles I've endured with my body. I spent years hating my body, and I hope my children do not carry that cross during their lives. But if they do, I will help them in whatever way I can. I know it's not entirely up to me, but I will do everything in my power to guard my children's hearts against the brokenness of this world.

I am especially worried for my daughter, my beautiful, fragile daughter. I was so excited when I found out that my second child was a girl. I imagined her wearing lots of pretty pink dresses and playing with dolls and decorating her room with princesses and fairies. I envisioned bringing her to princess movies and Disney on Ice and going off on girls' weekends and women's retreats with her. I had our whole relationship already imagined, but now that she's here and she's getting older, I'm afraid for her. She's just so innocent and lovely, and I don't want to see her broken.

Though I know that I can't protect her from the world completely, I can make our home a safe place for her. I can teach her to love her body, and to treat it with the respect it deserves. I can show her what that means by setting a good example. I will not criticize my own body in front of my children. I will not criticize anyone else's body in front of my children. I will certainly never criticize my children's bodies. I will make every effort to always speak about the body in positive terms. I will not use food or exercise as punishment. I will not adopt any crazy diets, and I will teach my children the benefits of the virtues of temperance and self-discipline. Our yes does not mean much if we are unable to say no to the choices that are offered to us. I will do my best to keep my children healthy by ensuring they grow up in a healthy home.

I will also do what I can to affirm my daughter's femininity. She will be raised in a world that tells her that femininity is a weakness, and that if she wants to be taken seriously, she needs to act more like a man—she needs to be strong and stoic and most likely dress in semi-masculine pantsuits. She will grow up in a world that will encourage her to use her femininity as a tool to get what she wants from men, that will define her according to the size of her jeans or her bra. I do not want her to believe the lies that the world will tell her.

I want her to know that a girl can be gentle and strong at the same time, that she can enjoy dresses and pink, but also like getting dirty and playing with trucks. I want her to know that it's OK if she wants to become a doctor or a lawyer or a teacher or a homemaker. I want her to believe that her femininity is a gift to be cherished and never a burden to be carried or a tool to be used. I want her to know that she is beautiful, inside and out, and that the size of her jeans or her bras will never detract from her beauty. I want her to believe with all her heart that she is perfect just the way God made her. She is incredibly beautiful just the way she is, and there is no need for her to change. The world might want to teach her otherwise, but I hope that she will always know the truth. She is God's perfect masterpiece.

QUESTIONS FOR REFLECTION

1. What does modern media tell our young girls and boys about themselves and their role in this world? What are the positive and negative consequences of such an attitude?

The Great Gift of Motherhood

2. What can Mary reveal to us about what it means to be a mother?

3. Why do we refer to Mary as "mother of the Church"?

4. How are women in particular called to be co-creators with God?

5. What are some ways that we can teach young girls to love their bodies?

An Exercise in Seeing Yourself as God Does

LEADING BY EXAMPLE

In this chapter, we discussed the importance of raising the next generation of women to have healthier, more peaceful relationships with their bodies. Children receive messages about their bodies at a variety of levels throughout their lives, including those modeled for them by others, explicit messages at home and in their community, and society-level messages spread through media. Consider some of these strategies for supporting healthy relationships with food and body at each level. Add your own ideas!

WHAT CAN I DO AS AN INDIVIDUAL?

• Be compassionate and loving toward your body.

• Focus on flexibility and moderation in eating rather than rigid food rules (e.g., avoid saying "good" foods and "bad" foods).

• Let children see you challenge unhelpful messages about food and bodies.

WHAT CAN I DO IN MY HOME OR COMMUNITY?

- Encourage children to develop a sense of self rooted in their identity as adopted children of God.

- Reframe language to talk about function rather than appearance (e.g., "how does your body serve you?" instead of "how does your body look?").

- Keep "fat" talk out of your home.

- Compliment people of all body shapes and sizes.

- Encourage participation in activities and hobbies to help build a sense of mastery and competence.

- Foster meaningful relationships with others not rooted in appearance.

HOW CAN I MANAGE SOCIETAL MESSAGES ABOUT BODIES?

- Talk explicitly with children about the messages they are exposed to, especially through social media.

- Limit exposure to social media where appropriate.

- Point out harmful messaging in media that children may be consuming.

- Expose children to media figures of all shapes and sizes.

Conclusion

About six months into writing this book, I found myself standing in front of a group of twenty or so teenagers, giving a talk on Mary. We had already gone through the bulk of the session, and the floor was open for questions. A young woman raised her hand and asked, "Did Mary experience pain when she gave birth?" I told the young woman that no, I did not believe that Mary felt pain while giving birth because she had been immaculately conceived. She was without sin, and pain in childbirth was the result of sin. But the girl's question led me into an incredibly eye-opening tangent (for me and for them).

I proceeded to tell the group that while I was confident Mary had suffered no physical pain during childbirth, there were other elements of the pregnancy and childbirth experience I was less certain about. Did her ankles swell at the end of a long day on her feet? Did her skin shine with that pregnancy glow? And most importantly, did Mary have stretch marks? I told them that these were the questions I was considering for a book that I was writing. Another hand shot into the air. "What is your book about?"

So I told them. I told those girls all about this book, this journey of healing that I walked and wrote down. And as I talked, I watched them. I saw how they leaned forward hungrily. I saw how they nodded along enthusiastically, because they knew exactly what I was talking about. I saw how their eyes lit up in understanding, and hope, and joyful expectation. And I saw how they looked at each other, realizing for the first time that maybe they were not alone in their struggles and desires. Nearly that whole room of girls hungered for the same thing. They wanted peace with their bodies. They wanted to read my book. They wanted to find healing in Christ.

My heart broke as I looked around that classroom. So many hungry girls. So many souls who were spiritually starving. So many beautiful, broken hearts. In a very unique way, this book is for them. I finished this book because of their encouragement, and because of their need. But this book is also for me, because sometimes I forget where I came from and where I am going. I forget that my body is a gift, the physical manifestation of the beautiful work of art that I am. I forget that I am more than just a number on the scale, or on the tag of my jeans, or in the cup of my bra. I forget that I am perfect just the way God made me, that I am fearfully and wonderfully made, and that God created me as his perfect masterpiece.

This book is for every girl who has ever felt that she was not enough, that she wasn't pretty enough or smart enough or thin enough. This book is for every woman who has looked in the mirror and forgotten what God sees when he looks at her. This book is for every girl who has hated her body, punished herself, or desperately chased after a form of perfection that is impossible. This book is for every woman who has been broken and is seeking Christ's healing. This book is for all of you.

LEARNING TO BE PATIENT WITH YOUR BODY

When I was eight months pregnant with my first child, people began to warn me that I would need to be patient with my body after the birth. They liked to tell me that since it took nine months to put all the weight on, it would take *at least* ten months to lose it. They also seemed to assume that I *would* get my "old body" back sooner or later, and that this was a goal worth achieving. The first time around, they were right about the timetable they had given me. By the time my son turned one, I looked about the same as before my pregnancy, but with deeper bags under my eyes. I had retired my pregnancy wardrobe for my old jeans and tops. A few months later, I was pregnant again, and I assumed the timetable would be the same the second time around.

In a way, I was right. By the time my daughter turned one, I was happy with how I felt. But my body still looked different. My old jeans still didn't fit. Even though my eating and exercise habits had not changed, my body had, and it refused to change back. I realized that despite my best efforts, my body wasn't going to go back to what I considered normal. I needed a new normal. And I needed new jeans.

Pregnancy and childbirth change you forever. That becomes more and more true with every pregnancy. After my first pregnancy, I just relied on eating well and daily stroller naps, and after a few months, I looked as I had before getting pregnant. That was simply not true after my second child was born. I worked out and ate well, but my body still felt very different. After fighting my new normal for a while, I realized this was a battle I didn't want to fight anymore.

In the end, the number on the scale didn't matter. The size of my jeans didn't matter. My kids didn't love me any less. My husband didn't love me any less. So I decided not to love my body any less. I was proud of my body, proud of what it had done to give life to my children, and I was proud of myself for developing the self-discipline and temperance necessary to live happily and healthily. I was happy and healthy. Why should I care about the size of my jeans or the number on the scale? I was happy with how I felt and proud of what I had done in my life. Why should I allow myself to be discouraged?

It's been nearly a decade since I hit rock bottom and began the long, difficult journey of recovery. I found healing in the most absurd of places—while I was pregnant, swollen, and weighing more than I had ever weighed in my life. But I also felt beautiful, and happy, and healthier than I had probably ever been in my life. I was living for my son, making choices for the health of my child. And after months of healthy living, I didn't want to go back to my pre-pregnancy habits. Some habits are meant to be broken. Some changes are good. The changes to my mental and physical health were good. And the changes to my body were good too.

Motherhood has made me a better woman. Becoming a mom taught me healthy habits for eating and exercising. Motherhood has encouraged me to love my body and to marvel at its abilities. I am proud of my body now. But that doesn't mean I don't fall back into bad habits from time to time. Sometimes the temptation to judge myself harshly, to berate myself for my so-called flaws, wins out. Sometimes I listen to the lies. I let myself be defeated. But then I get back up again. I might lose a battle from time to time, but I will not lose the war, not when I have Christ on my side.

LEARNING TO LOVE YOUR BODY

About a year after my daughter was born, I was still getting used to my new body. I had embraced my new stay-at-home mom wardrobe, which was made up of loads of leggings, T-shirts, hoodies, and athletic shorts. I claimed that my wardrobe shift was due to my new role as a homemaker, but I had also embraced my new clothes as a convenient way to hide my body. I was not yet comfortable with its new shape, and I felt best when my new curves were hidden beneath layers of forgiving fabric. I was still struggling to embrace the changes motherhood had wrought on my flesh.

On one particular evening, I found myself pulling a T-shirt over my head when my husband walked into our room. I quickly yanked it down to cover my stomach. He came over to wrap his arms around my waist, preventing me from completing my task. Then he said something that completely shifted how I viewed my body.

"Why do you want to hide your stomach? I love your stomach." In that moment, I felt just a little bit like Eve facing God right after the Fall. "Why did you hide?" he asked me. "I saw that I was naked, so I hid myself," I told him. But why do I feel like I need to hide? Why do we feel like we need to hide from those who love us most? As I looked at my husband, I knew that he was telling the truth. He did love my stomach. He loves my entire body. He loves me, and he loves every part of me. And if that's how much my husband loves me, how much one fallen human being loves another, how much more must God love me?

I am still learning to love my body. It's going to be a lifelong journey, but this is a path that I'm happy to be walking. I need to learn to love my body the way that my husband loves it, the way God loves it. I need to trust that when my husband tells me I'm beautiful, he's telling me the truth. I need to believe that God is speaking through my husband, reminding me of the truth I've forgotten. I am fearfully and wonderfully made. I have been fashioned with love and care. I have been created by the divine artist, and I am God's beautiful masterpiece. And so are you. We all are.

Acknowledgments

This book is about fifteen years in the making, and there are just so many people who have helped *See Yourself as God Does* come to life. To all those who have accompanied me on my own journey of healing, thank you. This book certainly wouldn't be here without you. To my classmates and professors at the John Paul II Institute, thank you for giving me the words that I needed to embrace my body as the gift from God that it is. To the young women I met back in 2020 at Sacred Heart of Jesus Church, thank you for encouraging me to share my past. Meeting you was truly the impetus I needed to start writing. If it hadn't been for you, this book would probably still be a mess of thoughts in my head.

To everyone at Ascension, and especially to Hadleigh Thomas, thank you for accompanying me on my journey to becoming a real author. You have made this whole process a breeze, and it has been an honor to work with all of you. Thank you to Rick and Marie Dooley for suggesting that my husband pitch a book to Ascension. I doubt that you had any idea that you had two future Ascension authors sitting in your living room that night. Thank you to all the family and friends who have helped me write this book, for the babysitting offers and celebratory meals. It has been such a blessing to share this all with you.

To Mom and Dad, thank you for always encouraging me in my writing and supporting me as I worked to become "mom" and "writer" at the same time. To my children, John and Felicity, thank you. Becoming your mother has forever changed the way I see my body. Thank you for always seeming to know when I needed time to write and for always playing so nicely together during those times. To John, who loves to tell me that I look pretty, and to Felicity, who proudly tells anyone who will listen that she is beautiful, thank you. I pray that you will always think that of yourself, my sweet girl. And to my loving husband, Andrew, thank you. When I forget how beautiful I am in the eyes of God, you always remind me. You loved my body even before I learned to really love it. Marrying you and raising our family has been the most amazing adventure of my life. I am so grateful that we got to share the journey to becoming published authors as well. I couldn't have done any of this without your love and support.

And finally, to God, who has never given up while trying to get his message across. Even during my lowest moments, I never doubted you were there with me. You sent me so many people to love me and help me to see myself the way you see me. You never gave up on me, and now I can confidently say with the psalmist, "I am wondrously made" (Psalm 139:14). Thank you for giving me the strength and grace to seek the true Healer and to share my story in these pages. This book is a product of your grace and love for me. Thank you, Lord.

Further Reading

To dive even deeper into any of these topics, see the following posts on my blog, loveinthelittlethingsblog.com:

"God Wants Us to Be Perfect, Not Perfectionists," April 12, 2021

"Dear Daughter, Don't Let the World Break You," November 9, 2020, originally printed at herviewfromhome.com

"Christianity and Mental Illness," April 20, 2020

"How I've Come to Embrace My Body: Rediscovering a Healthy Body Image," February 24, 2020

"Motherhood and the Healing of Body Image and Eating Disorders," December 9, 2019

"'I Believe in ... the Resurrection of the Body,'" January 29, 2018

"How Pregnancy and Childbirth Taught Me to Love My Body," March 7, 2016

"The Self-Destructive Habits of the Perfectionist and Its Link to Pride," March 23, 2015

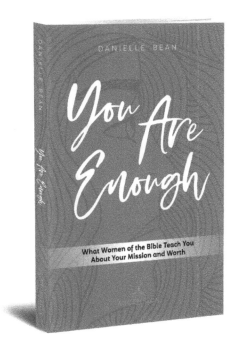